WORLD ENGLISH 3

Real People • Real Places • Real Language

Kristin L. Johannsen / Rebecca Tarver Chase

HEINLE
CENGAGE Learning™

Australia • Brazil • Japan • Korea • Mexico • Singapore • Spain • United Kingdom • United States

World English 3
Real People • Real Places • Real Language
Kristin L. Johannsen
Rebecca Tarver Chase

Publisher: Sherrise Roehr

Managing Editor: Berta de Llano

Senior Development Editor: Margarita Matte

Development Editor: Michael Poor

National Geographic Editorial Liaison:
  Leila Hishmeh

Technology Development Manager:
  Debie Mirtle

Director of Global Marketing: Ian Martin

Director of US Marketing: Jim McDonough

Product Marketing Manager: Katie Kelley

Marketing Assistant: Jide Iruka

Senior Content Project Manager/Art Direction:
  Dawn Marie Elwell

Senior Print Buyer: Betsy Donaghey

Compositor: Nesbitt Graphics, Inc.

Library of Congress Control Number: 2008937885

International Edition:
World English 3 ISBN 13: 978-1-4240-5016-1
World English 3 ISBN 10: 1-4240-5016-2
World English 3 + CD-ROM ISBN 13: 978-1-4240-5104-5
World English 3 + CD-ROM ISBN 10: 1-4240-5104-5

U.S. Edition:
World English 3 ISBN 13: 978-1-4240-6338-3
World English 3 ISBN 10: 1-4240-6338-8

Heinle
20 Channel Center Street
Boston, MA 02210
USA

Cengage Learning is a leading provider of customized learning solutions with office locations around the globe, including Singapore, the United Kingdom, Australia, Mexico, Brazil, and Japan. Locate your local office at:
international.cengage.com/region

Cengage Learning products are represented in Canada by Nelson Education, Ltd.

Visit Heinle online at elt.heinle.com

Visit our corporate website at www.cengage.com

Printed in Canada
1 2 3 4 5 6 7 13 12 11 10 09

CONTENTS

	Unit Goals	Grammar	Vocabulary	Listening	Speaking and Pronunciation	Reading and Writing
UNIT 1	**People and Places** page 2 • Discuss reasons for living where you do • Explain why people stay or leave where they live • Describe a new place • Examine human migration	Present perfect tense vs. present continuous tense *She **has moved** three times in her life.* *It**'s been raining** all day* So + adjective + that *It's so dry here that water is brought in on trucks.*	Migration Climate	Focused listening Interviews about why people live where they do	Discussing reasons for staying or moving Contractions with *have* and *be*	"Pioneers of the Pacific" Writing a traveler's journal
UNIT 2	**The Mind** page 14 • Talk about remembering and forgetting • Talk about your senses • Talk about your fears • Describe an emotional experience	Gerunds as subjects and after prepositions ***Learning** English is important.* *We talked about **studying** together.* May, might, and *could* for possibility *We **may** find dangerous animals in the jungle.*	Thought processes Scientific investigations	Listening for general understanding and specific information A radio program about the unusual condition of synesthesia	Talking about sensations *Th* sounds	"In Your Face" Writing about a personal experience
UNIT 3	**Changing Planet** page 26 • Discuss causes and effects • Suggest solutions to the climate change problem • Understand the complex problem of invasive species • Consider the ways present actions affect the future	Passive voice—all tenses *The cookies **were eaten**.* Past perfect tense *By the time sea level **had risen** ten feet …*	Environmental changes Large numbers	General and focused listening Climate change	Discussing cause and effect Linking words	"The Carbon Connection" Writing a letter about life in the future
UNIT 4	**Money** page 38 • Describe your money habits • Discuss things that people value • Talk about banking • Talk about wealth	Gerund vs. infinitive *I try **to make** a budget./* *I enjoy **finding** bargains.* Review of the passive voice *Coffee **is grown** in Brazil.* *That movie **was made** by two teenagers.*	Money transactions Banking	General and focused listening Radio program: The history of money	Giving suggestions for how to have fun for free Reduction of *to*	"Big Winners—or Big Losers?" Writing a personal opinion
UNIT 5	**Survival** page 50 • Talk about emergency situations • Evaluate survival methods • Consider animal survival • Describe a survival school	Unreal conditional *If they weren't inside the shelter, they would quickly die.* Wish *I **wish** I had brought a good book to read in the shelter.*	Survival skills Environmental conservation	Listening for general understanding A radio program interviewing survivors	Simulation: working with a team in a survival situation Reduced sounds: *didja* and *d'ya*	"Survival Schools" Writing an advertising brochure
UNIT 6	**Art** page 62 • Report what another person said • Express your opinions about art • Describe your favorite artists and their art • Talk about public art	Reported speech: statements *She said she was tired and her head hurt.* Subject adjective clauses *An artist **who works with clay** has strong hands.*	Art terminology Art materials	Listening for general understanding Conversations in a museum	Discussing personal selections Quoted and indirect speech	"Saving a City's Public Art" Writing a detailed description

	Unit Goals	Grammar	Vocabulary	Listening	Speaking and Pronunciation	Reading and Writing
UNIT 7	**Transportation** page 74 • Talk about new developments in transportation • Talk about choices in transportation • Use English to get around • Make recommendations for improving transportation	Passive voice: present continuous tense and present perfect tense *The new plane **is being tested** now./Computers **have been used** for more than 50 years.* Indirect questions ***Do you know** where the bus stop is?*	Modern transportation Public transportation	Focused listening A discussion: Subway systems	Role-play: Solving an airport problem Reduced *are*	"The Rickshaws of Kolkata" Writing a letter to the editor
UNIT 8	**Competition** page 86 • Give your opinion about sports • Choose the best sport for your personality type • Talk about positive and negative aspects of competition • Discuss competitive advantages	Negative questions ***Isn't** that dangerous?* Object adjective clauses *It's a competition **that she often wins**.*	Sportsmanship Sports	Listening for general understanding and specific information Interviews	Matching sports to personalities Rising intonation for surprise	"In Sports, Red is the Winning Color" Writing a list of competition tips
UNIT 9	**Danger** page 98 • Discuss ways to stay safe • Talk about dangerous work • Discuss personal emergencies • Discuss taking risks	Tag questions *Those spiders are poisonous, **aren't they**?* Adverbial clauses of time *I finished my project **before I went home**.*	Dangerous things Expressions for emergencies	Focused and general listening Radio program: An unusual job	Role-play: A newspaper interview Intonation of tag questions	"A Delicacy to Die For" Writing about a risk situation
UNIT 10	**Mysteries** page 110 • Speculate about mysteries • Discuss types of mysteries you like and dislike • Talk about plans you used to have • Explain a mysterious Image	Modals for speculating about the past *He **might** have seen a large fish instead of a sea monster.* Future in the past *The two sisters **were going to** have a picnic by the lake.*	Reactions to surprise Investigating mysteries	Listening for general understanding Interviews of eye-witnesses	Role-play: Two sides of a mystery—belief and disbelief Intonation of tag questions	"Hands Across Time" Writing about fauxtography
UNIT 11	**Learning** page 122 • Talk about educational plans and decisions • Discuss your learning style • Talk about choosing a university major • Propose a new approach to teaching	*Should have, could have, would have* *I **should have** applied for a scholarship.* Noun clauses ***What you said** was very interesting.*	Education University majors	Listening for general understanding Personal experiences	Discussing quiz results Past modals	"Game-Filled Park is School for South African Kids" Writing about improving schools
UNIT 12	**Space** page 134 • Talk about the future • Consider the realities of living in space • Discuss the future of space exploration • Summarize a sequence of events	Future tenses with *will* and *be going to*, simple present tense, present continuous tense Future modals *We**'ll be able to** see it from here.*	Space exploration Future time expressions	General and focused listening Interview of an astronaut	Role-play: Choosing a space experiment Stress in compound nouns	"The Hubble Space Telescope" Writing about orbiting telescopes

Get To Know

San Francisco, California, USA
Immigrants to San Francisco's Mission District give the neighborhood its heart and its art. *San Francisco's Mission District*

United States of America
Meet the men and women who spend their days breaking things—in order to keep people safe. *Destroyers*

New York City, New York, USA
Speed, danger, and escaping from the police are a part of their job every day. *Big City Bicycle Messengers*

Texas, USA
Move over, cowboys! These women rodeo champions excel in the toughest sport in the American West. *Women in the Rodeo*

Hawaii, USA
Find out what brings astronomers to the top of the world's highest volcano—Mauna Kea in Hawaii. *Comet Watchers*

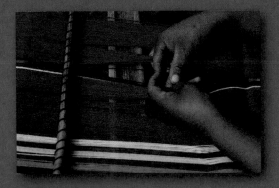

Chinchero, Peru
High in the Andes Mountains of Peru, traditional crafts provide a new road to economic survival. *Andean Weavers*

Your World!

England, United Kingdom
They appear overnight in England's quiet farm country. Who or what creates these circles in the corn? *Crop Circles*

England, United Kingdom
To become a real English butler, men and women from around the world must learn some unusual lessons. *Butler School*

The Netherlands
In the Netherlands, climate change and rising sea levels are on everyone's mind. Is it time to stop fighting against nature? *The Netherlands: Rising Water*

Fes, Morocco
In the traditional markets of Morocco, the first price you hear isn't always the real price. *Making a Deal*

Italy
He can remember every word in more than 200 books and everything that ever happened in his life. How does he do it? *Memory Man*

Australia
One traditional art in Australia may be more than 40,000 years old. *Rock Art*

= Sites of the video clips you will view in *World English 3* .

PEOPLE AND

1. Where are the people in the pictures?

2. Why do you think people live in these places?

UNIT GOALS

Discuss reasons for living where you do
Explain why you plan to stay or leave
Describe a new place
Examine human migration

Vocabulary

A. Read the questions and answers. Notice the words in blue.

> Why do people move to new places? Long ago, **ancient** people wanted to **inhabit** places with plenty of food and other resources. These people got food in the same ways we do now: farming, **hunting** or **herding** animals, or **fishing** if they lived near water.
>
> Because of competition for food, over-crowding was one reason early people moved. They sometimes walked very long distances or rode on animals, but they had to **sail** across water.
>
> Nowadays, modern people may move in search of **employment** or a better climate. The **migration** of large groups of people may **occur** because of economic problems or a lack of food or water. **Political** problems can also cause people to migrate.

B. Write the words in **blue** next to their meanings.

1. to live in a place _____
2. moving across water in a boat using the wind _____
3. catching fish _____
4. moving from one part of the world to another _____
5. killing wild animals for food _____
6. having a job _____
7. very old; from an earlier time _____
8. caring for a group of animals such as cattle or sheep _____
9. to happen _____
10. relating to the way power is achieved or used in a society _____

Grammar: Present perfect tense vs. present perfect continuous tense

Present perfect tense *have* + past participle	**Present perfect continuous tense** *have* + *been* + present participle
We use the present perfect tense to talk about things: *that began in the past and continue now. *Professor Brown* **has spoken** *Swahili since he was a child.* *that have happened several times. *She* **has moved** *three times in her life and she plans to move again next year.* *that happened at an unspecified past time and are connected with the present. *I've* already **eaten** *breakfast, so I'll just have some coffee, please.*	We use the present perfect continuous tense to emphasize that something which began in the past is unfinished or temporary. *I've* **been working** *on this assignment all afternoon, and I'm still not finished.* *Laura* **has been staying** *with her cousins while her parents are in Europe.* *how long something has been in progress. *It's* **been raining** *all day.*

Complete the sentences. Use the present perfect or present perfect continuous form of the verb in parentheses.

1. Can we rent a different movie? I _____ (see) that one already.
2. We _____ (bake) cookies since ten o'clock this morning!
3. Hurricanes _____ (occur) in this region only four times in the last 100 years.
4. Our teacher _____ (live) in five countries, so he's not surprised by different beliefs and customs.
5. I can't find my dictionary, so I _____ (use) my friend's dictionary this week.
6. George _____ (try) to find a better job, but so far, he hasn't found one.

Conversation

Track 1-2

A. Listen to the conversation. What does Sonia like about the place where she lives?

Jacob: Do you like living here?

Sonia: Sure. Don't you?

Jacob: I guess so, but I've been reading about a lot of interesting places, and I've been thinking about moving someplace else.

Sonia: Well, this is a pretty interesting place, too. People have lived here for a long time because it's a good place to live.

Jacob: Why do you say that?

Sonia: It's near the ocean, for one thing, so there's always fresh seafood.

Jacob: That's true.

Sonia: And the weather is usually nice. It's never very cold, and we don't get serious storms very often.

Jacob: OK, but is it really an interesting place?

Sonia: I think so. Hey, let's go to the historical museum. We can find out about some of the fascinating things that have happened here.

 B. Practice the conversation with a partner. Switch roles and practice it again.

✔ Goal 1   **Discuss reasons for living where you do**

Tell a partner why you live where you live. Has your family lived there for a long time? What do you like and dislike about living there? Have you ever moved to a new place?

Listening

 A. What are the most important reasons for living in a certain place?
Rank the reasons below (1 = most important) and add two more reasons.

_____ the climate

_____ having family members nearby

_____ employment opportunities

_____ one's ancestors lived there

_____ environmental quality (clean air, water, etc.)

_____ _____

_____ _____

Track 1-3 **B.** Listen to four people talk about the places where they live.

▲ Speaker #1   ▲ Speaker #2   ▲ Speaker #3   ▲ Speaker #4

Engage!

Do people move more than they used to? What are some advantages of moving to a new place? What are some advantages of staying in the same place?

Track 1-3 **C.** Listen to each speaker again and answer these questions.

	Where does the speaker live?	Why does the speaker live there?	Does the speaker plan to move?
Speaker #1			
Speaker #2			
Speaker #3			
Speaker #4			

Communication

 A. Interview your partner and take notes on his or her answers.

Why do you live where you live?	
How are your reasons different from your parents' or grandparents' reasons?	
What might make you want to move to a new place?	

Pronunciation: Contractions with *have* and *be*

Track 1-4

A. English speakers often use contractions with auxiliary verbs. Listen to the pronunciation of *have* and *has*. Listen again and repeat the sentences.

I have never been to Africa.   I've never been to Africa.
Ron has written two books.   Ron's written two books.

Track 1-5

B. Listen to the full and contracted forms of *be*. Listen again and repeat the sentences.

Tanya is moving to Singapore.   Tanya's moving to Singapore.
We are paid twice a month.   We're paid twice a month.

 **C.** Work with a partner. Change the full forms of *have* and *be* to contractions and then practice saying the sentences.

1. We have been living in Beijing for seven years.
2. Marsha is planning to visit us in December.
3. I am going to give her a call tonight.
4. They have never stayed in the same place for more than two years.
5. We are taking the train from Nairobi to Mombasa.
6. I have always wanted to go there.

Real Language

To *give someone a call* means to call someone on the telephone.

✓ Goal 2   Explain why you plan to stay or leave

In a small group, find out how many people plan to move someday. Ask those people to explain why they want to go to a new place. Ask the people who don't want to move to give their reasons for staying in the same place.

Language Expansion: Climate

A. Match the adjectives with the places on earth they describe. Use your dictionary to help you.

tropical	places that receive very little rain
temperate	places that receive a large amount of rain
snowy	places with distinct seasons that are never extremely hot or cold
rainy	places that receive a large amount of snow
arid	extremely cold places
frigid	hot, humid places near the earth's equator

B. With a partner, fill in the blanks with places on earth that fit the descriptions.

1. _____ has a tropical climate.
2. _____ has a temperate climate.
3. _____ has a snowy climate.
4. _____ has a rainy climate.
5. _____ has an arid climate.
6. _____ has a frigid climate.

Grammar: *So + adjective + that*

NG MAPS

So + adjective + *that*

*We use *so* + adjective + *that* to explain that:
(1) a condition is quite extreme and (2) that it has a result.

Condition	Result
*He was **so** tired*	***that** he fell asleep when his head touched the pillow.*
*The climate is **so** dry here*	***that** water is brought in on trucks.*

A. Complete the conversation. Use *so* + adjective + *that*.

Mia: How was your trip to Ghana?

Daniel: Great! But Ghana has a tropical climate, so it's hot all the time.

Mia: Really? How hot was it when you were there?

Daniel: It was _____ I didn't mind taking cold showers every day. It also rained a lot while I was there.

Mia: How rainy was it?

Daniel: It was _____ I carried my umbrella everywhere I went. The people in Ghana were very friendly, though, so I didn't mind the weather.

Mia: That's good. How friendly were they?

Daniel: Many of them were _____ they invited me to their homes for dinner right after they met me. I ate some wonderful home-cooked meals!

B. Complete the sentences with any appropriate adjective.

1. Yesterday, I was very _____.
2. In January, my country is very _____.
3. Before an important test, most students are very _____.
4. The climate in Antarctica is very _____.
5. Someday, I will be very _____.

 C. Take turns. Say a sentence from exercise **B**. Then ask questions using *how* and answer them with *so* + adjective + *that*.

How happy were you?

I was so happy that I couldn't stop smiling.

Conversation

 A. Listen to the telephone conversation. How has Ryan's life changed recently?

Track 1-6

Sandra: How's it going, Ryan? Are you getting used to your new home?

Ryan: I'm all right. It's a very big city, though, so it takes forever to get anyplace.

Sandra: Really? What about the new subway system? Isn't it fast?

Ryan: The trains are fast, but they're so crowded that sometimes you have to wait for the next one. I can take buses, of course, but they make a lot of stops.

Sandra: I see what you mean.

Ryan: Fortunately, I love my new job, and it's right downtown.

Sandra: That's nice! You can walk around on your lunch hour.

Ryan: That's exactly what I've been doing! I've been looking for good restaurants.

Sandra: That's great! You know I like trying new restaurants.

Ryan: That's right. When you visit me, I'll know where to take you to eat.

 B. Practice the conversation with a partner. Switch roles and practice it again.

C. Continue the conversation. Use your imagination to ask and answer questions about:

the climate where Ryan lives now
the people who live there
Ryan's new job

Real Language

When you *get used to* something, it becomes normal for you.

You can say that something *takes forever* when it feels like a very long time.

 **Goal 3**   **Describe a new place**

Imagine that you've been living in a new place for a few weeks. Where are you? Tell a partner about your life in your new home.

▲ a modern Hawaiian voyaging canoe built on ancient designs

Reading

 A. Find answers to these questions in the reading.

1. When did the Lapita migration occur? _____

2. Where did the Lapita voyages begin? _____

3. How far into the Pacific did the Lapita people travel? _____

4. What aspect of Lapita culture came from the Philippines? _____

5. In which direction do the trade winds usually blow? _____

6. How does El Niño affect the trade winds? _____

B. After you read, talk to a partner about possible answers to these questions.

1. Do you think the Lapita people came from one place in Asia or from several different places? Why?

2. Why do you think the Lapita left their homes and sailed to Pacific Islands?

3. What might archaeologists find in a cemetery that would help them to understand an ancient culture?

4. How might the Lapita have sailed so far and located so many islands without modern equipment?

☐ South Pacific

Pioneers of the Pacific

No one is sure how they did it or even why they did it, but over 3,000 years ago people sailed into the enormous emptiness of the Pacific Ocean in simple **canoes**. Within a few centuries, these people—now known as the Lapita—had migrated from the volcanoes of Papua New Guinea to the island of Tonga, at least 2,000 miles to the east. They explored millions of square miles of the Pacific, and they discovered and then inhabited dozens of tropical islands never before seen by human eyes: Vanuatu, New Caledonia, Fiji, Samoa.

There is much we do not know about the Lapita. Although their **voyages** began in the northern islands of Papua New Guinea, their language came from Taiwan, and their style of pottery decoration probably had its roots in the northern Philippines. So who were the Lapita? Did they come from a single point in Asia or from several different places?

Now, archaeologists Matthew Spriggs and Stuart Bedford of the Australian National University are working to answer these questions. A Lapita **cemetery** on the island of Éfaté in the Pacific nation of Vanuatu has revealed information about Lapita customs, and DNA from the ancient bones may help to

▲ canoe

answer questions about the Lapita people. "This represents the best opportunity we've had yet," says Spriggs, "to find out who the Lapita actually were, where they came from, and who their closest descendants are today."

But even if the archaeologists can answer those questions, we still won't know how the Lapita sailed so far east against the trade winds, which normally blow from east to west. Atholl Anderson, professor of prehistory at the Australian National University, suggests that El Niño, the same warming of ocean water that affects the Pacific today, may have helped. Climate data obtained from slow-growing corals around the Pacific and from lake-bed **sediments** in the Andes of South America indicate a series of unusually frequent El Niños around the time of the Lapita expansion. By reversing the regular east-to-west flow of the trade winds for weeks at a time, these *super El Niños* might have carried the Lapita sailors on long, unplanned voyages far over the horizon.

However they arrived on the islands, the Lapita came to stay. Their descendants have inhabited the region for thousands of years, and why not? They're living in an island paradise that many of us only dream about.

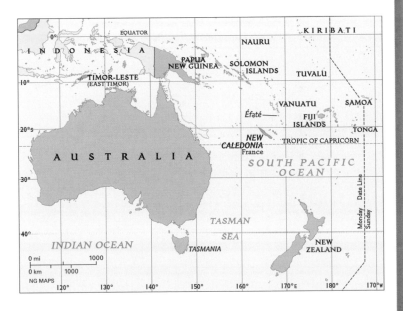

Word Focus

voyage = a long journey on a ship
cemetery = a place where dead people's bodies are buried
sediment = soil that has settled to the bottom of a body of water

Communication

People move or migrate for many different reasons. *Pull* reasons are things that attract people to a new place. *Push* reasons make people want to leave their homes. Fill in the chart with several possible reasons for the Lapita migration.

Factors that *pulled* the Lapita to the Pacific	Factors that *pushed* the Lapita from their original homes

Writing

What was life like for the Lapita people? Use your imagination. Write one page from the journal of a Lapita explorer.

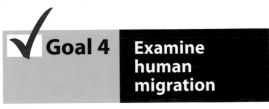

✓ **Goal 4** **Examine human migration**

Imagine moving with your family to another country. Tell a partner why you would ever do this. Where would you go? What would it be like?

Before You Watch

 A. Discuss these questions with a partner.

1. What do you know about San Francisco, California?
2. What might attract immigrants to that city?
3. When immigrants come to live in a new place, what parts of their culture do they bring with them?

B. Read about the video and check the meanings of the words in **bold**.

In 1791, people from Spain began to build a **mission**, a kind of religious **community**, in the place that later became San Francisco. Nowadays, San Francisco's Mission District is an interesting and **multicultural** neighborhood. Local residents and immigrants from many countries feel **comfortable** living here. The cultures and **traditions** of **Latin America** are especially easy to see and hear in the **murals** and the music of this special place.

▲ the Golden Gate Bridge in San Francisco

While You Watch

 A. Watch the video and match the people with their roles.

1. Ray Patlan ____   a. mural artist
2. Juan Pedro Gaffney ____ b. priest at Saint Peter's Church
3. Father Dan McGuire ____ c. director of the Spanish Choir of San Francisco

 B. Read the video summary and fill In the blanks with words from the box. Then watch the video again and check your answers.

churches arts Spanish Central special integration

Video Summary

In this video, we can see that the Mission District is special in several ways. Religion has played a role in the community since the _____ arrived. Today, large _____ such as the Mission Dolores Basilica are places where new immigrants can practice their religious traditions. Music is another thing that makes the neighborhood _____. The Spanish Choir of San Francisco has performed to raise money for people after natural disasters in _____ America. In this way, they are able to be involved with countries in Latin America, where some of the singers still have family and friends. The visual arts also make the Mission District a special place. One street called Balmy Alley is famous for its murals, and a local _____ organization leads people on walking tours through the area. At the end of the video, a priest explains that the _____ of the best parts of different cultures makes the Mission District a beautiful place.

After You Watch

A. If you lived in the Mission District, what would you enjoy about the neighborhood?

B. How does the neighborhood where you live or where you go to school compare to the Mission District? Use a T-chart to list similarities and differences.

Similarities	Differences

Communication

Pretend you are going to make a video about the neighborhood where you live or where you go to school. What parts of the neighborhood will you show in the video? What people will you show or talk to? What will the narrator say?

THE MIND

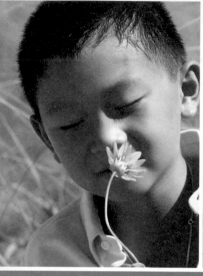

1. Which senses are the people in
   the pictures using?
   a. sight
   b. smell
   c. taste
   d. hearing
   e. touch

2. Which sense is the most important for you?
   Why?

UNIT GOALS

Talk about remembering and forgetting
Talk about your senses
Talk about your fears
Describe an emotional experience

Vocabulary

A. Read the article. Match the words in **blue** with their meanings.

A Bigger Brain

Every day, Glen McNeill rides his motorbike around London for seven hours. He wants to become a taxi driver, so he must **memorize** every street in the city and then pass a test called "The Knowledge of London." He will answer questions about 400 routes between important places. It's an incredible test of **memory**. The examiner names two places and candidates must **react** quickly and give the names of every street and landmark along the route between those two places.

Preparing for the exam takes three years, and passing it is extremely difficult. Some people try as many as 12 times. McNeill and the other *Knowledge Boys* (and *Knowledge Girls!*) use many different **techniques** for studying at home. They **visualize** all the places on a route to make a **mental** map. They also **concentrate** on remembering street names that sound similar.

Now scientists have discovered important differences in these drivers' brains. The **portion** of the brain that **retains** information about places is larger in London taxi drivers than in other people. Learning "The Knowledge" might make their brains grow new **cells**.

1. memorize ___	a. a way to do an activity
2. react ___	b. keep, continue to have
3. technique ___	c. the smallest part of an animal or plant
4. visualize ___	d. make a picture in your mind
5. mental ___	e. your ability to remember things
6. concentrate ___	f. think very hard about something
7. portion ___	g. part
8. retain ___	h. in your mind
9. cell ___	i. to speak or move when something happens
10. memory ___	j. to learn so that you can remember exactly

 B. Discuss the questions with a partner.

1. Do you think you would be successful as a *Knowledge Boy* or *Girl*?
2. What would you do to learn all the streets of London?

Engage!

What was the most difficult exam you have ever taken? How did you prepare for it?

Grammar: Gerunds as subjects and after prepositions

A gerund is a noun formed from a verb + *ing*.

ask → *asking*   sit → *sitting*   try → *trying*

Gerunds can be used as the subject of a sentence.
Saying *new vocabulary words is a good way to remember them.*
Learning *English is important for my future.*

Gerunds can be used after a preposition.
I'm interested <u>in</u> **becoming** *a taxi driver.*
We talked <u>about</u> **studying** *together.*
He's afraid <u>of</u> **flying** *on airplanes.*

A. Find five gerunds in the article about taxi drivers. Tell a partner why each one was used.

B. Complete each sentence with the gerund of a verb from the box.

| memorize   get   travel   ride   forget   lose |

1. _____ all the streets for the taxi drivers' exam takes three years.
2. Jackie is interested in _____ to China to learn about Chinese history.
3. I worry about _____ my friends' birthdays. They feel bad when I don't send them a card.
4. For Glen McNeill, _____ his motorbike is the best way to learn about London.
5. I sometimes think about _____ a new job where I can use my English.
6. I'm afraid of _____ my wallet, so I always keep it in the same place.

 C. Tell your partner about good ways to do these things. Use gerunds.

| remember birthdays   practice listening to English   get more exercise |

Conversation

A. Listen to the conversation with your book closed. What did Diane forget?

Track 1-7

Katie: Hi, Diane. You don't look very happy.

Diane: I'm not. I had an important business meeting this afternoon, and I completely forgot to bring my laptop. My boss was really upset.

Katie: Everybody forgets things sometimes. You shouldn't worry about it.

Diane: I have such a terrible memory!

Katie: Making a list is a good way of remembering things. That always helps me.

Diane: But I'll just forget about the list!

Katie: If you put it on top of your keys, you'll see it when you go out. That's what I always do.

B. Practice the conversation with a partner.

C. Talk about things these people can do to remember. Then make new conversations with a partner.

1. A student has to learn 100 words for a vocabulary test.
2. The president of a neighborhood association can't remember the names of all the members.

 Goal 1   Talk about remembering and forgetting

Talk to a partner about remembering something that is important to you. What is it? How do you remember it? What happens if you forget?

Word Focus

Other common combinations of verb + preposition:

**worry about
look forward to
plan on
be tired of
think about**

Listening

 A. Discuss these questions with a partner.

1. What's your favorite song? Why do you like it?
2. When you listen to the song, does it make you think of any of these things?
   a person   a color   an experience   a place   a season   a picture

B. Listen to a radio program about an unusual brain condition called *synesthesia*. Circle the answers.

Track 1-8

1. When a person has synesthesia, two kinds of (memories/senses) work together.
2. Lori Blackman is unusual because she always sees (letters/sounds) in different colors.

C. Listen again. Circle **T** for *true* and **F** for *false*.

Track 1-8

1. The word *synesthesia* comes from the Greek words for *together* and *senses*.	T	F
2. There are two different kinds of synesthesia.	T	F
3. Lori's father has synesthesia, too.	T	F
4. Some artists and musicians have synesthesia.	T	F
5. Lori has a lot of problems because of synesthesia.	T	F

D. Listen again and fill in the information.

Track 1-8

1. The most common kind is called _____ synesthesia.
2. Lori realized she was unusual when she was _____ years old.
3. For Lori, B is light _____.
4. About one person in _____ has synesthesia.

E. Discuss the questions with a partner.

1. Do you know someone who has had experiences like this?
2. Would you like to have synesthesia? If so, what kind? If not, why not?

Pronunciation

Track 1-9

A. *Th* has two pronunciations in English—voiced and unvoiced. Listen and repeat the words and notice the pronunciations of *th*.

Voiced *th*	Unvoiced *th*
the	think
this	three
that	theater

B. Say these words. Decide which /th/ sounds are voiced and which are unvoiced.

> **thousand those Thursday they thank thief thirsty them**

C. Read the sentence. Which words have voiced *th*? Which words have unvoiced *th*? Say the sentence out loud as fast as you can.

I thanked that thin thief for the three theater tickets.

Communication

Look at the pictures. Imagine you are in these situations. What can you see, hear, smell, taste, and feel? Describe as many details as you can. Use your imagination!

> I feel warm sand under my feet. I smell the ocean.

✓ **Goal 2 Talk about your senses**

Work with a partner. Imagine you are in your favorite place in the world. What can you see, hear, smell, taste, touch, and feel right now?

Language Expansion: Scientific studies

A. Study the words about science and their meanings.

laboratory—a place where scientists work
research—studying something to discover new facts about it
theory—a scientific idea
survey—collecting information by asking many people the same questions
experiment—a scientific test to see if something is true
results—the information that scientists get after an experiment
compare—see how two things are similar or different
conclusion—something you decide after looking at all the information

B. Read the article. Complete the sentences with words from exercise **A**.

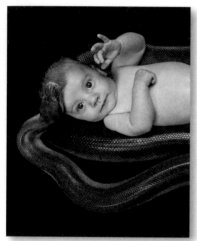

Our Biggest Fear

Everyone is afraid of snakes—right? An old _____ says that fear of things like snakes and fire is built into our brain, because animals that are afraid of dangerous things live longer and have more babies. But some scientists have done _____ that shows that we might learn to be afraid of things.

Scientists did an interesting _____ with monkeys to see if this is true. They _____ two groups of monkeys. One group of monkeys was born in the jungle, and the other group was born in a _____ at the university. They put the two groups of monkeys together, and showed them videos of snakes. At first, the jungle monkeys were afraid of the snake videos, but the laboratory monkeys didn't react. Then the laboratory monkeys saw that the jungle monkeys were afraid of snakes, and they became afraid too. These _____ show that monkeys learned about fear and dangerous things from watching other monkeys. The researchers' _____ was that fear is partly built into monkey's brains, but it is activated by watching other monkeys.

Scientists think that people could develop a fear of snakes in the same way, because babies are not afraid of them. In any case, the fear of snakes is very powerful. In one _____, 51 percent of people said that snakes are their biggest fear!

 C. Discuss the questions with a partner.

1. Are you afraid of snakes? Why, or why not?
2. Are you afraid of any other animals? Explain your reasons.

Grammar: *May, might,* and *could* for possibility

May, might, could		
We	**may**	find dangerous animals in the jungle.
Monkeys	**might**	learn to be afraid of things.
People	**could**	develop a fear of snakes.

*We use *may, might,* and *could* + base verb to say that something is possible, now or in the future.
*We also use *may, might,* and *could* to express that we are not completely sure about something:
   *Scientists say that other fears **are** learned.* (= the scientists are sure about this)
   *Scientists say that other fears **might be** learned.* (= the scientists are not sure about this, but it's possible)

A. Why are these people afraid? Complete each sentence with *may*, *might*, or *could* and a phrase from the box.

get on the wrong train	**see a snake**	**have an accident**
need a filling in my tooth	**fall off**	**make a mistake**

1. I don't like to walk across high bridges because <u>I could fall off.</u>
2. Jose Luis is afraid of speaking English because _____
3. My grandmother gets nervous when she's driving because _____
4. I don't like camping because _____
5. Nancy never takes the subway because _____
6. I worry about going to the dentist because _____

 B. What are you afraid of? Tell your partner, and explain the reasons with *may*, *might*, or *could*.

Conversation

Track 1-10

A. Listen to the conversation with your book closed. What is Andy afraid of?

Susan: You look really nervous, Andy. What's up?
Andy: Oh, I always feel like this before I take a trip. I hate flying!
Susan: Really? But you travel a lot!
Andy: I never feel comfortable. The plane might fly into bad weather, or the pilot could make a mistake.
Susan: I used to be afraid of flying too, but I got over it.
Andy: Really? How?
Susan: Listening to music on the plane makes me feel calm.

Real Language

When you *get over* a bad experience or an illness, you recover from it.

 B. Practice the conversation in exercise **A** with a partner. Then make new conversations about these things. Use your own ideas for ways to get over these fears.

✓ Goal 3 Talk about your fears

Tell your partner about something you're afraid of. Why are you afraid of it?

Reading

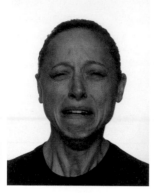

A. Discuss these questions with a partner.

1. What happened to each person in the photos? Why do they feel like this?
2. What makes you feel these emotions?

B. Circle **T** for *true*, **F** for *false*, and **NI** for *no information* (if not in the reading).

1. Paul Ekman studied people's faces in different cultures.   T F NI
2. Ekman did research in several countries and got different results.   T F NI
3. Americans get angry more often than the Fore people from New Guinea.   T F NI
4. Ekman thinks that emotions are the same everywhere because they are a part of our brain.   T F NI
5. Two people might feel different emotions about the same thing.   T F NI
6. Fear is the most difficult emotion to change.   T F NI

San Francisco, California, USA

In Your Face

Why is this man so angry? We don't know the reason, but we can see the emotion in his face. Whatever culture you come from, you can understand the feeling that he is expressing.

Forty years ago, psychologist Paul Ekman of the University of California, San Francisco, became interested in how people's faces show their feelings. He took photographs of Americans expressing various emotions. Then he showed them to the Fore people, who live in the jungle in New Guinea. Most of the Fore had never seen foreign faces, but they easily understood Americans' expressions of anger, happiness, sadness, disgust, fear, and surprise.

Then Ekman did the same experiment <u>in reverse</u>. He showed pictures of Fore faces to Americans, and the results were similar. Americans had no problems reading the emotions on the Fore people's faces. Ekman's research gave powerful support to the theory that facial expressions for basic emotions are the same everywhere. He did more research in Japan, Brazil, and Argentina, and got the same results. According to Ekman, these six emotions are <u>universal</u> because they are built into our brains. They developed to help us <u>deal with</u> things quickly that might hurt us. Some emotional triggers are universal as well. When something suddenly comes into sight, people feel fear, because it might be dangerous. But most emotional <u>triggers</u> are learned. For example, two people might smell newly cut grass. One person spent wonderful summers in the country as a child, so the smell makes him happy. The other person remembers working very hard on a farm and being hungry, so he feels sad.

Once we make an emotional association in our brain, it is difficult, and sometimes impossible, to change it. "Emotion is the least changeable part of the brain," says Ekman. But we can learn to manage our emotions better. For instance, we can be more aware of things that make us angry, and we can think before we react.

There are many differences between cultures, in their languages and customs. But a smile is exactly the same everywhere.

C. Look back at the reading and think about the meaning of the underlined words. Circle the answers.

1. If you do something *in reverse*, you do it again (the same way/the opposite way).
2. If something is *universal*, it's (the same/ different) in every country.
3. When you *deal with* a problem, you (take action/don't think about it).
4. An emotional *trigger* makes an emotion (happen/stop).

Communication

Think about a time when you felt one of the emotions in the reading. Tell your partner about your experience. Your partner will ask you for more details.

1. What happened?
2. How did you feel?
3. What did you do?
4. What did you learn from this experience?

Writing

Write about the experience that you described in the Communication activity. Be sure to include lots of details about the experience and your feelings.

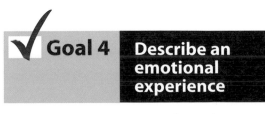

Goal 4 **Describe an emotional experience**

Share your writing with another partner or the entire class.

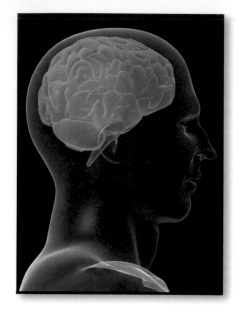

Before You Watch

 A. How good is your memory? Study one of these lists of numbers for two minutes. Then close your book and try to say the list to your partner. Your partner will check. How many numbers did you remember correctly?

List A: 14   89   7   463   26   1987   115   74
List B: 391   70   22   1850   34   208   9   16

B. Read the information and study the words in **bold.**

> **How does memory work?**
>
> When we get new information, it goes into a part of the brain called the **hippocampus.** There the information is **coded** and put into memory. But why are some people better at remembering? Some scientists think a good memory comes from **heredity.** We get it from our parents through their **genes.** Other people say a good memory comes from practice.

While You Watch

 A. Watch the video. Choose the main idea.

a. Having a good memory can make your life easier.
b. Scientist are trying to find out why some people have good memories.
c. Some families in Italy have very good memories.

 B. Watch the video again. Complete the sentences.

1. Gianni Golfera is blindfolded but he can still show these people something that's _____.
2. He has memorized more than _____ books.
3. Researchers are now studying how memory and _____ change the brain.
4. For Gianni, improving his memory has become almost like a _____ _____.
5. Gianni's life is not all about _____, though.
6. Gianni's practice and hard work are making his memory _____ _____.

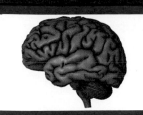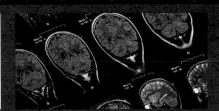

C. Watch the video a third time and circle the answers.

1. Gianni Golfera has an excellent memory for ___.
   a. words and numbers   b. things that happen   c. both **a** and **b**
2. Scientists __ why some people have very good memories.
   a. know exactly   b. don't understand   c. have some ideas about
3. Scientists think that Gianni's unusual memory might be the result of ___.
   a. hard work   b. his parents' teaching   c. good genes
4. Gianni thinks his unusual memory is the result of ___.
   a. hard work   b. his parents' teaching   c. good genes

After You Watch

Discuss the questions with a partner.

1. Why do you think Gianni Golfera has such a good memory?
2. Would you like to take Gianni's memory class? Explain your reasons.

Communication

Follow the steps to play a famous memory game.

1. With your group, choose 12 small objects such as a pencil, key, comb, ruler, and so forth. Arrange them on top of a desk and cover them with a big piece of paper.
2. With your group, go to another desk. Take away the sheet of paper. In one minute, try to memorize the objects you see. Then put the paper back.
3. Work individually for two minutes to list all the objects you can remember.
4. Go back to the other desk with your group and check your list. Then discuss the game with your group. Who remembered the most objects? What strategies did you use to memorize them? What did you learn about your memory?

CHANGING

1. What words best describe each picture?
   a. coal
   b. deforestation
   c. a flood
   d. polar ice

2. In what ways have human beings changed the environment?

UNIT GOALS

Discuss causes and effects

Suggest solutions to the climate change problem

Understand the complex problem of invasive species

Consider the ways present actions affect the future

PLANET

Vocabulary

A. Read an article from an environmental magazine.

> **A New Mother Earth?**
> The Earth is changing fast—with a little help from people. Our use of coal and **oil** for energy has led to **global warming**. This warming has led to an **increase** in **temperatures** and **sea levels**, and much less polar ice. But warming is not the only effect we have on the planet. **Climate change** means more **extreme** weather of all kinds: heat, cold, rain, and drought.
>
> The effects of human activity can also be seen in the planet's plant and animal life. Demand for tree products and farmland leads to **deforestation**, and our tendency to travel all over the globe provides easy transportation for **invasive species**—plants and animals that are brought in, sometimes accidentally, from other places.
>
> Fortunately, these problems are well-known, so even though we humans are the cause, we can also be part of the solution. We can use much less coal and oil if we practice **conservation**, for example, and better land management means that forests don't have to be destroyed. Invasive plants and animals can even be controlled, but only with a good understanding of the environment.

B. Write the words in **blue** next to the correct meanings.

1. a thick liquid found underground and used as a fuel _____
2. very great in degree or intensity _____
3. the cutting down of trees over a large area _____
4. how hot or cold something is _____
5. saving and protecting the environment _____
6. the number, level, or amount becoming greater _____
7. a gradual rise in the earth's temperature _____
8. the average level of the ocean _____
9. plants and animals with no local natural controls on their populations _____
10. a change in the normal weather patterns _____

Grammar: Passive voice—all verb tenses

Active voice	Passive voice	Passive with *by*
Subject + transitive verb + direct object	Direct object + *be* + past participle of transitive verb	Passive + *by* + agent
The children **ate** the cookies.	The cookies **were eaten**.	The cookies were eaten **by the children**.

We use the passive voice:

*when the agent (the doer) is unknown or unimportant: *The store was robbed last night.*
Our apartment is painted (by painters) every three years.

*to emphasize the object of the verb: *Our neighbor's apartment hasn't been painted in a long time.*

Using the *by* phrase

*The *by* phrase is used to indicate the agent in a passive sentence.
*Data is being collected **by researchers** from Brazil.*

A. Write answers to the questions using the passive voice. (You might need to guess.)

1. Where is tea grown? _____
2. When was the telephone invented? _____
3. How is electricity produced? _____
4. What can be done to stop global warming? _____
5. Why have invasive species become a problem? _____

B. Complete the sentences with any appropriate agent.

1. Those nests in that tree were made by _____.
2. This textbook was published by _____.
3. Oil is being used as fuel by _____.
4. My favorite kind of shampoo is made by _____.
5. Rising sea levels are caused by _____.

Communication

 A. How do these things happen? Match the causes of environmental changes with their effects.

Causes	Effects
1. burning coal and oil	a. rising sea levels
2. deforestation	b. invasive species
3. movement of people and goods	c. pollution in the atmosphere
4. climate change	d. fewer trees
5. increasing temperatures	e. more extreme weather

 B. Get together with another pair of students and compare answers. Does everyone agree? Discuss different ways to look at causes and effects.

> Air pollution is the effect of burning coal and oil.

> That's true, and air pollution also causes increasing temperatures.

✓ Goal 1   Discuss causes and effects

Make a list of things you do every day that affect the environment. Then explain your list to the class.

Listening

 A. Rank these types of extreme weather from most serious (1) to least serious (5).

_____ floods

_____ very cold weather

_____ hurricanes/typhoons

_____ drought

_____ very hot weather

B. Listen to four people talk about climate change. Write the name of a place below each picture.

Track 1-11

1. _____ 2. _____ 3. _____ 4. _____

 C. Listen again. Answer each question.

Track 1-11

1. According to Mari, what is happening to the cattle?
2. How many deaths occurred in Europe during one heat wave?
3. Why do some scientists say that global warming isn't causing the heat waves?
4. According to Joseph, how many hurricanes and tropical storms occurred one year?
5. How does warm ocean water cause strong storms?
6. How are recent floods in Jasmine's country different than in the past?

Pronunciation: Linking words together

> **Linking Words Together**
>
> Linking makes spoken English smoother. When a word ends in a consonant sound and the next word begins with a vowel sound, the words are linked together.
>
> *What's the capital of Japan?* (Can you hear the word *love* when you say this?)
>
> When a word ends in a consonant sound and the next word begins with the same consonant sound, the words are linked and the sound is only pronounced once.
>
> *We didn't feel like going home, so we went to the museum.* (Can you hear *fee-like* and *wen-to* when you say this?)

 A. Underline the sounds that link together. Then listen and check your answers.

Track 1-12

1. Climate change has been in the news lately.
2. Do you know how to make coffee?
3. Please stand up.
4. I'm not sure when to use the past tense.
5. The governor is worried about food shortages.
6. What time do you usually get up in the morning?

 B. Write complete sentences using these word pairs. Then practice saying the sentences.

1. waste time
2. turn over
3. some milk
4. large jackpot
5. boiled egg
6. brighter rainbow

Conversation

 A. Close your book and listen to the conversation. What does Pedro think should be done about climate change?

Track 1-13

Sonia: Hey, what's up? You look worried.
Pedro: I am worried.
Sonia: About what?
Pedro: I hear a lot about climate change, but I feel like nothing is being done about it.
Sonia: I know what you mean, but what do you think should be done?
Pedro: Well, look at this neighborhood. More trees could be planted.
Sonia: Would that help?
Pedro: Definitely! Trees keep cities cooler, so they don't become heat islands.
Sonia: Heat islands! I learn something new every day.

 B. Practice the conversation with a partner. Switch roles and practice it again.

✓ **Goal 2** **Suggest solutions to the climate change problem**

Discuss with classmates how climate change is affecting your country. Make a list of ways people in your country could help solve the climate change problem. Share your list with the class.

Language Expansion: Large numbers

Saying Large Numbers

To say large numbers in English, start at the left, and say the numbers in groups:

hundreds (100s)	524 → five hundred (and) twenty-four
thousands (1,000s)	1,250 → one thousand, two hundred (and) fifty
ten thousands (10,000s)	17,400 → seventeen thousand (and) four hundred
hundred thousands (100,000s)	432,060 → four hundred thirty-two thousand (and) sixty
millions (1,000,000s)	2,400,900 → two million, four hundred thousand (and) nine hundred

 A. Discuss these questions with a partner.

1. What are invasive species? Can you think of an example?
2. Why are invasive species a problem?

B. Read about Macquarie Island. Guess which number is correct.

Macquarie Island, Australia ®

Like many places, Macquarie Island had invasive species—species of nonnative plants and animals with no local natural controls on their populations. First came the cats, which were used on ships to control rats. Then came the rabbits, which were brought by seal hunters as a source of food. The hunters came because Macquarie Island is visited by around **(8,000/80,000/800,000)** elephant seals each year. No hunting is allowed now, however, because the island is a wildlife sanctuary.

Macquarie Island has also been an accidental sanctuary for its invasive species. The rabbits found plenty to eat, and they ate an enormous amount of the island's plant life. In 1968, scientists wanted to decrease the rabbit population, so the European rabbit flea (which carries a virus called myxomatosis) was introduced. By the 1980s, the rabbit population had declined from **(1,300/13,000/130,000)** to only **(2,000/20,000/200,000)**, and the vegetation on the island had begun to recover. But with fewer rabbits to eat, the cats began to prey on the island's sea birds, so scientists decided to kill the island's cats.

Problem solved? Unfortunately, the virus had only reduced the rabbit population, and with the cats gone, the rabbits' numbers increased again. Now, so much of the island's vegetation is gone that there have been landslides after heavy rains. One expert estimates that it will cost **($162,000/$1,620,000/$16,200,000)** to finally solve the invasive species problem on Macquarie Island.

Answers: 80,000; 130,000; 20,000; $16,200,000

What do you think? 8,000 or 80,000 or 800,000?

I think it's 8,000.

 C. Take turns asking about the numbers in the article.

Grammar: Past perfect tense

Past perfect tense: subject + *had* + (*not*) + past participle

* We use the past perfect tense to talk about something that happened before a specific past time.
* We often use the past perfect tense with *by* + a certain time.
  *I **had finished** all of my homework **by 8:00** last night.*
* The simple past tense is often used instead of the past perfect tense with words such as *before* or *after* when the time relationship is clear.
  We ate dinner before the program started.

A. Read each sentence and underline what happens first.
1. Cats had already arrived when the rabbits were brought to the island.
2. By the time Penny got home, her brother had eaten all of the strawberries.
3. I intended to do the laundry, but someone had done it earlier.
4. James called his mother after he finished playing soccer.
5. The rabbit population had increased dramatically by 1968.
6. Before the sun went down, Rita found a good place to watch the fireworks.

B. Read the article about Macquarie Island again and underline the verbs in the past perfect tense. Why is the past perfect tense used in those sentences?

Conversation

Track 1-14

A. Close your book and listen to the conversation. What does Henry want to do?

Abdullah: Look at this, Henry.
Henry: Eeeew . . . What is it?
Abdullah: I'm not sure. It's some kind of insect, but I've never seen one like it.
Henry: Maybe it came here on a ship or something—in a box of food.
Abdullah: Right! The ship had probably been to another country to pick up . . . kiwi fruit!
Henry: Kiwi fruit? Alright. And after it picked up the fruit, the ship came here.
Abdullah: And now our country will be invaded by the terrible Australian Kiwi Beetle!
Henry: Not if we do something about it first.
Abdullah: Hold on, Henry. We can't kill it if we don't even know what it is.
Henry: You're right. Maybe we should show it to Ms. Becker, the biology teacher.

 B. Practice the conversation. Then switch roles and practice it again.

✓ Goal 3   Understand the complex problem of invasive species

Discuss one or two invasive species you know about. Why is it difficult to get rid of these plants or animals?

Reading

 A. Discuss these questions with a partner.

1. Are you optimistic or pessimistic about the future?
2. Do you think people will solve the problem of global warming?

 B. Find the information in the article.

1. What are the effects of global warming?
   _____

2. How much has the earth's temperature risen? _____

3. What kind of power plant produces the most carbon? _____

4. What are three examples of sustainable energy sources? _____

5. How do forests reduce the amount of carbon in the air? _____

Word Focus

greenhouse effect = atmospheric warming caused by gases such as carbon dioxide that keep heat from escaping into space

emissions = gases and other substances that are released into the atmosphere

sustainable = able to be continued for a long time

bio-fuels = a plant substance that is burned for heat or power

☐ Earth

The Carbon Connection

We don't agree on everything, but the world does seem to agree on one thing: Global warming is happening, and it's causing big problems. And the biggest cause of global warming is carbon in the form of carbon dioxide produced by burning coal and oil.

Carbon dioxide in the atmosphere keeps heat from escaping into space. Long ago, this **greenhouse effect** was a good thing. It kept the earth from becoming too cold. But in modern times, more carbon dioxide has been entering the atmosphere, so less heat can escape. We've already raised the earth's temperature over one degree Fahrenheit, and we can see the devastating effects—melting polar ice, retreating glaciers, severe weather, and changes in sea life.

The solution is to burn less, but with the earth's population growing, how can this be accomplished? The answer, according to experts, is not one amazing new technology, but rather all of the existing technologies combined.

Clean electricity Coal-burning power plants produce much of the carbon that enters the atmosphere. If we use natural gas or nuclear energy in all new power plants, we will greatly reduce carbon **emissions**. Coal can also be converted to a clean-burning gas before it is used to produce electricity.

There is also technology that captures the carbon produced by burning coal so that it can be stored underground.

Sustainable energy Energy for heating and electrical power can also come from **sustainable** sources. Large *wind farms* with dozens of wind turbines can be seen in many parts of the world. Thousands more wind turbines would decrease the world's carbon emissions, and we will never run out of wind, unlike coal or oil. Solar panels are another investment in the future, along with **bio-fuels** from corn, soybeans, sugar cane, and grasses.

Forest protection Trees have the ability to remove carbon dioxide from the atmosphere, but unfortunately, they're disappearing fast. Forests are logged to meet the construction industry's demands for wood, and trees are cleared to make room for farming, which only increases the amount of carbon in the air. Protecting forests, on the other hand, leads to a better environmental future.

Conservation Using less energy to begin with may be the easiest way for most of us to decrease carbon emissions. Switching from old-fashioned incandescent light bulbs to high-efficiency fluorescent lights dramatically decreases our electrical consumption. Lifestyle changes are also important, for example, turning off computer monitors when we're not using them and riding bicycles or using public transportation. Finally, if all new buildings, appliances, and vehicles were designed with energy efficiency in mind, we could stabilize or even decrease the amount of carbon entering the atmosphere.

Communication

A. On the left side of the chart, write three things you will do today to help prevent future global warming.

1.	
2.	
3.	

 **B.** Share your list with a partner. Discuss the effects your three actions will probably have. On the right side of the chart, write phrases and key words to help you remember your discussion.

Writing

The year is 2099. Write a letter to an ancestor who lived in the early part of the 21st century. Tell your ancestor what the world is like in 2099. Explain how the three things he or she decided to do back then have affected the world of the future. Use the information from your chart.

✓ **Goal 4** | **Consider the ways present actions affect the future**

Talk to a partner. Pretend that one of you is optimistic about the future and one of you is pessimistic. Explain how the things people are doing now will (or will not) solve the problem of global warming.

Before You Watch

A. Read the information about the Netherlands and check the meaning of the words in **bold**.

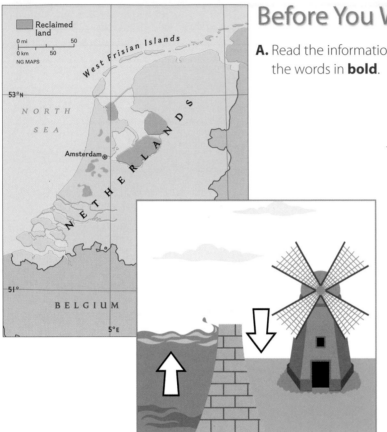

The Netherlands—Quick Facts

- Another name for the Netherlands is Holland.
- About half of the country's land is below sea level.
- The Dutch (people from the Netherlands) have built walls of earth called *dikes* between the sea and the land. These dikes have created new areas of dry land.
- Windmills are used to move water from the land to the sea, and as the water is removed, the land **sinks** even lower.
- As sea levels **rise** due to global warming, the Dutch must decide how to deal with the rising water. Should they continue to **struggle** against the sea?

B. How do you feel about water? Check the sentences you agree with.

1. ____ Lakes and rivers are beautiful places for recreation.
2. ____ The sea can be managed and controlled.
3. ____ If I lived in the Netherlands, I would worry about floods.
4. ____ I would like to live near a body of water.
5. ____ I'm interested in the idea of a floating house.
6. ____ I like to visit lakes or the sea, but I wouldn't want to live near water.

 C. Explain your ideas about water to a partner.

While You Watch

 A. Watch the video and choose the best phrase to complete each sentence.

1. Instead of fighting the sea, it might be necessary to _____.
   a. struggle against the sea   b. give land back to the sea
2. Flood control lakes could be used for _____.
   a. recreation and wildlife   b. farmland
3. Older Dutch people don't like the idea because they think _____.
   a. fighting the water is necessary   b. water makes a pretty landscape

▲ Dutch windmills use the energy of wind to move water.

 **B.** Watch the video again. Complete the information from the video with numbers.

1. Global warming is expected to cause the sea level to rise between _____ inches and _____ feet this century.
2. _____ to _____ percent of the country's land was created by man, pumping water out from marshlands.
3. Today more than _____ people live below sea level on land that only stays dry because of the constant work of pumps and dikes.

 C. Talk about the statistics in exercise **B**. Why is each fact important?

After You Watch

 Discuss with a partner. What are the advantages of letting some of the land in the Netherlands fill up with water? What might some of the disadvantages be?

Communication

Divide your group into two smaller groups. Imagine that the people in one group own farmland or a house near water in the Netherlands. They are concerned about flooding. The other people agree with the idea from the video. They want the Netherlands to stop fighting the sea. Role-play a discussion between the two groups of people.

▲ a canal in Amsterdam

MONEY

1. Which of these forms of money do you use most often? Why?

2. How many different currencies can you name? Which countries are they from?

UNIT GOALS

Describe your money habits
Discuss things that people value
Talk about banking
Talk about wealth

Vocabulary

A. Read the statements below. Mark your opinions.

This week's Opinion Survey
What are your thoughts?

MONEY

	Agree	Disagree
1. People should only **borrow** money if they want to buy something really big, like a car.	_____	_____
2. It's always a bad idea to **lend** money to your friends.	_____	_____
3. I try to make a **budget** for how I will spend my money.	_____	_____
4. I prefer to pay in **cash** when I buy things.	_____	_____
5. It's OK if young people are **in debt** because they can pay back the money when they are older.	_____	_____
6. For me, a good **income** is more important than an interesting job.	_____	_____
7. I'm very careful with my money and I enjoy finding a **bargain** when I go shopping.	_____	_____
8. My living **expenses** are very high.	_____	_____

B. Write the words in **blue** next to their correct meanings.

1. money in coins and bills _____
2. to get money that you will give back in the future _____
3. money that you spend _____
4. a plan for spending your money _____
5. to give money to another person that they will give back in the future _____
6. money that you receive for working _____
7. something good for a low price _____
8. owing money to a bank or a company _____

C. Compare your answers in exercise **A** with a partner's answers. Explain your reasons.

Grammar: Gerund vs. infinitive

Verb + infinitive

We use infinitives after certain verbs, including

   hope   try   want   learn   need   promise   decide   agree

I **try to make** a budget for how I will spend my money.

Verb + gerund

We use gerunds after certain verbs, including

   avoid   enjoy   stop   finish   give up   consider

I **enjoy finding** a bargain when I go shopping.

Verb + infinitive or gerund

We can use infinitives or gerunds after certain verbs, including

   like   prefer   hate   begin   continue   love

I **prefer to pay** in cash. Or I **prefer paying** in cash.

A. Complete the sentences with the infinitive or gerund of the verb in parentheses.

1. I decided _____ (save) money for a new computer.
2. Mark agreed _____ (work) on Saturdays so he can have Mondays off.
3. I stopped _____ (eat) in restaurants, and I learned _____ (cook) simple meals.
4. Loren hopes _____ (study) in Australia next year.
5. If you are in debt, you should avoid _____ (borrow) more money.
6. I'm trying _____ (get) a different job so I can have a higher income.

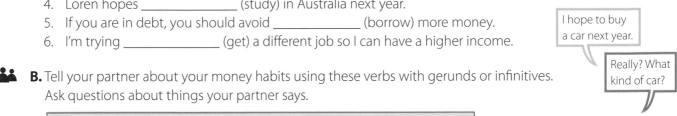

 B. Tell your partner about your money habits using these verbs with gerunds or infinitives. Ask questions about things your partner says.

| I love . . .   I hope . . .   I decided . . .   I stopped . . .   I usually avoid . . . |

Conversation

Track 1-15

A. Listen to the conversation with your book closed. When does the man go out with his friends?

Beth: I love eating in restaurants, but it's so expensive now!

Rick: Yeah, I know. That's why I stopped going out for dinner. I meet my friends on Saturday at noon, because lunch is a bargain at lots of places.

Beth: That's a good idea.

Rick: We like to eat in small, neighborhood restaurants. They're not so expensive.

Beth: And they usually have better food.

Rick: I think so, too. And one more thing—I avoid having dessert. That's another good way to save money.

Beth: You don't have dessert? That's a little too extreme for me!

 B. Practice the conversation with a partner.

 C. With your partner, list three ideas for how to save money on each of these things. Make new conversations.

food   clothes   vacations

D. Share your money-saving ideas with the class.

Goal 1   Describe your money habits

Are your money habits similar to your friends' habits or different? Tell a partner.

Listening

A. Listen to a radio program about the history of money. Circle the main idea of the program.

Track 1-16

1. People have used many different things as money.
2. People's ideas about money have been the same for thousands of years.
3. Money causes different problems in people's lives.

B. Listen again and number the places on the map in the order that you hear about them.

Track 1-16

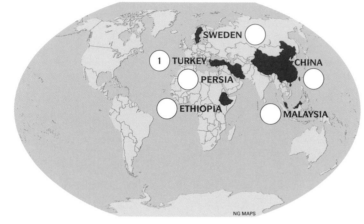

SWEDEN

1 TURKEY   CHINA

PERSIA

ETHIOPIA   MALAYSIA

NG MAPS

C. Listen again. Circle **T** for *true* and **F** for *false*.

Track 1-16

1.	Coins were made in Turkey about 3,000 years ago.	T	F
2.	Paper money is older than coins.	T	F
3.	The people in Persia liked to use paper money because it was new.	T	F
4.	Coins and bills are the only kinds of money.	T	F
5.	The Indians in North America had a form of money.	T	F

D. Discuss these questions with a partner.

1. Why do people want money? Talk about as many reasons as you can.
2. Does having more money always make people happier? Explain your answer.

brass kettle

blocks of salt

cowries

wampum

Pronunciation: Reduction of *to*

Track 1-17

A. The word *to* is usually pronounced very quickly, with a /ə/ sound. Circle the word *to* in these sentences and then listen to the pronunciation.

1. The king told all the people to use paper money.
2. People began to use coins a long time ago.
3. I try to learn five English words every day.
4. I like to find a bargain when I go to the store.
5. He sent an email to his parents to ask them for money.
6. We go to the library after class.

B. Read the sentences in exercise **A** to a partner. Pay attention to the pronunciation of *to*.

Communication

A. Read the saying. What do you think it means?

The best things in life are free.

B. Make a list of things you enjoy that don't cost any money. Then share your list with a partner.

C. Your class is going to write a guidebook for people who want to have fun without spending money. Follow these steps.

1. With your group, list as many ideas as you can for fun activities that don't cost money.

Things to do at home	Things to do with your friends	Things to do in your city

2. Write your lists on the board.
3. With the class, choose the best ideas in each category

D. Which of the activities have you done? Which activities do you want to try?

✔ **Goal 2** **Discuss things that people value**

Work with a partner. Talk about things that people value in your country. Are these different now than in the past? Why, or why not?

Language Expansion: Banking

A. Label the pictures with words from the box.

| savings account | teller | PIN number | deposit | receipt | ATM | checking account | withdraw |

1. _____ 2. _____ 3. _____ 4. _____

5. _____ 6. _____ 7. _____ 8. _____

B. Which of the things in exercise **A** do you have experience with?

Grammar: Review of the passive voice

Passive voice	Subject + *be* + past participle (+ *by* agent)
Affirmative statement	Coffee **is grown** in Brazil (by farmers).
Negative statement	We **were not told** about the quiz (by our teacher).
Yes/no questions	**Are** credit cards **used** in your country?
Wh- questions	Where **was** that coin **made**?

*The passive voice can be used with any verb tense. Change the form of *be* to show the tense.

*Sentences in the passive voice talk mostly about the result of the action, not the person who does the action (the agent).

*The agent is included in the sentence only if that information is important or surprising.

    Hamlet *was written around 1601* **by William Shakespeare**. (important)

    That movie was made **by two teenagers.** (surprising)

A. Read the article and fill in the verbs in the passive voice. Be sure to use the correct tense.

How does an ATM work?

A man is on vacation in Paris, and he needs money from his bank in Washington. He goes to an ATM. In fifteen seconds, he receives 100 Euros from his savings account, and he can go out for a delicious dinner. How does this work?

The card _____ (insert) into the machine, and the PIN _____ (enter). The information _____ (send) to the bank's computer. The computer sees that it's a foreign ATM card, so an electronic message _____ (transmit) to the European computer banking center in Belgium, and then to the North American center in Detroit, and finally to the bank in Washington. The account _____ (check). If there is enough money in it, a message _____ (return) to the ATM in Paris, and the cash _____ (deliver).

ATMs _____ (invent) in the 1970s. At first, they _____ (not use) very much. Now they _____ (find) all around the world.

 B. Which of these sentences should include an agent? Why? Cross out the agent where it's not needed.

1. My computer was made ~~by factory workers~~ in Malaysia.
2. Our homework papers are collected every day by our teacher at the end of class.
3. I love to wear this dress because it was made by my grandmother.
4. While Alex was shopping in the Central Market, his wallet was stolen by a thief.
5. The telephone was patented in 1876 by Alexander Graham Bell.
6. The first paper money was used by the Chinese about 1,000 years ago.

Engage!

How often do you use an ATM? Why?

Conversation

Track 1-18

A. Listen to the conversation with your book closed. How much money does the woman want?

Teller: Next? May I help you?
Annie: Yes. I need to withdraw $100.
Teller: Please fill out this form and write your account number here.
Annie: OK.
Teller: Do you want to withdraw the money from your savings account or your checking account?
Annie: From my checking account, please.
Teller: Here you are, $100. And here's your receipt. Have a good day.
Annie: Thank you. You, too.

B. You want to do these things. Make new conversations.

deposit $200 in your checking account   withdraw $150 from your savings account

Real Language

Here you are. People use this expression when they hand something to someone.

Have a good day. Employees in banks and stores sometimes say this when they finish helping you. The response is *Thank you. You, too.*

✓ Goal 3   Talk about banking

When do you go to the bank? Talk about what you usually do there.

Reading

A. Discuss these questions with a partner.

1. Do you ever buy lottery tickets? Why, or why not?
2. If people win a lot of money, how do their lives change?

B. Read the statements. Circle **T** for *true*, **F** for *false*, and **NI** for *no information* (if the answer isn't in the reading).

1. Sheelah Ryan couldn't stay in her house after she won the lottery. T F NI
2. Sheelah gave a lot of her money to help other people. T F NI
3. Ed Kammen made good decisions about how to use his jackpot. T F NI
4. Ed and his wife still live in a large house today. T F NI
5. Many lottery winners lose their money in a short time. T F NI
6. Men have more problems than women if they win the lottery. T F NI
7. Family members cause problems for many lottery winners. T F NI

Florida, USA

Big Winners— or Big Losers?

Like most people, Sheelah Ryan sometimes bought lottery tickets, and, like most people, she never expected to win. Then one day she received astonishing news: She was the winner of $55 million, the biggest jackpot ever in the Florida State Lottery.

Her life changed overnight. She received more than 750,000 letters from people who wanted some of that wealth. She had to leave her home to escape from newspaper reporters, while friends stayed there to guard against thieves. After a few months, she bought a new house and car and then used most of the jackpot to start an organization that helps women and elderly people. Today, she is content with her life.

Not all lottery winners have such happy stories, however. Ed Kammen (not his real name) won $8.2 million 12 years ago in a state lottery. He lent money to family

members who were in debt and spent the rest of the money on a $5 million mansion. But he didn't plan for the expenses of such a big house. Taxes, insurance, and even furniture cost so much that he finally lost the house. His wife divorced him because of their financial problems, and he now lives alone in a small apartment.

In fact, nearly one-third of big lottery winners lose all their money in just a few years after their "big win." John Denny, a financial advisor, says too many people believe that money can solve all our problems. "But lottery winners soon find out that money also causes problems," he says. "If you were happy before you won, you will be happy afterwards too. But if you were an unhappy person, winning millions of dollars will only make things worse."

The biggest problem is friends and family members who demand help. Many lottery winners are pressured to put money into businesses that they don't understand, and they lose it all. Another problem is time. Winners usually quit working, but then they don't know what to do. "You can play golf for a few weeks," says Ed Kammen. "But you can't just play golf for 30 years!"

So, what should you do if you're a big winner? "Put your cash in the bank for a while," says John Denny. "Stop and think about what you really want in life and don't make any big decisions for a few months. And be sure to change your telephone number!"

C. Read the opinions and check the people from the reading who would say them. One, two, or three answers may be correct.

	Sheelah Ryan	Ed Kammen	John Denny
1. Wealthy people have a responsibility to help other people.			
2. Life is boring if you don't have a job.			
3. Winning a lot of money can make your life better.			
4. It's a bad idea to lend money to family members.			
5. If you are un-happy, having more money won't make you happy.			

Communication

A. Read the statements in exercise **C** again. Circle the numbers of the statements that you agree with.

B. Compare your opinions with a partner's opinions and discuss your reasons.

Writing

Choose one of the statements that you agree with or disagree with strongly. Write a paragraph about your opinion and explain your reasons.

✓ **Goal 4** **Talk about wealth**

How do people's lives change when they win the lottery?

Before You Watch

 You are going to watch a video about shopping in a marketplace in Morocco. What do you think people can buy there? List your ideas.

_____

_____

_____

▲ marketplace in Marrakech

While You Watch

 A. Watch the video *Making a Deal*. Circle the things from your list above that you see in the video.

 B. Watch the video again. Fill in the missing words in the sentences.

1. The souk in the city of Fes is Morocco's _____ market.

2. Across the alley, a man sells dates and apricots to hungry _____.

3. For the visitors, the question is not "_____ should I buy?" but "_____ should I buy it?"

4. However, visitors who want to practice making a deal here had better be _____!

5. This is where the sellers really pressure customers to buy _____.

6. Once you end up in a shop, you sit there drinking tea, and you say "I don't want to buy _____."

7. For some visitors to Fes, it may be difficult to leave without buying more than they _____.

 C. Watch the video again. Circle **T** for *true* or **F** for *false*. Correct the false sentences.

1. In the souk, only the seller decides the price. T F
2. Foreigners and Moroccans pay different prices in the market. T F
3. If you aren't good at bargaining, you might pay 10 percent more. T F
4. The vendors are trying to steal money from the shoppers. T F
5. The hat shop is the most difficult place for tourists. T F
6. Tourists can learn how to bargain by watching Moroccans. T F

After You Watch

 Discuss the questions with a partner.

1. Do you think bargaining for prices is a good system? Explain your reasons.
2. Have you ever bargained for something? Talk about your experience.

Communication

 Try *selling* something by bargaining! Follow these steps.

1. Choose something you have with you now, such as your watch, pen, or cell phone. Think of a description that will make it very attractive to a buyer, and decide on the price you would like to sell it for.
2. Show the item to a partner and describe it.
3. Bargain until you agree on a price.
4. Then change roles and "buy" something from your partner by bargaining.
5. Tell the class about the things you "bought" and "sold."

SURVIVAL

1. Which situation is the most dangerous?
   a. a fire
   b. adventure sports
   d. an earthquake
   e. rescue work

2. What can people do to survive in these situations?

UNIT GOALS

Talk about emergency situations
Evaluate survival methods
Consider animal survival
Describe a survival school

UNIT 5

▲ first-aid kit

Vocabulary

A. Read part of a survival brochure. Notice the words in **blue**.

> **Survival Advice**
> According to experts, there are several things you can do to increase your chances of survival in an **emergency**, such as a fire, or a **natural disaster**, such as an earthquake.
>
> - **Preparation** can be the key to survival. Be sure you have food, water, candles, and other **supplies** in your home. Having a backpack prepared for each family member is a good idea in case you have to **evacuate** quickly.
> - Before going camping, hiking, or mountain climbing, make sure you have the proper **equipment**. Tents, sleeping bags, and a **first-aid** kit can save your life in case of bad weather, injury, or illness.
> - Staying calm and taking the time to think can help you **cope** with any emergency **situation**. Swimmers, for example, sometimes get caught in strong ocean currents. If they **panic**, they may become exhausted and unable to swim. If they relax and swim slowly with the current, they will have the energy to swim to shore once they are out of the current.

Word Focus

To **cope with** a situation means to deal with it successfully.

 B. Discuss these questions with a partner.

1. What kind of natural disasters can happen where you live?
2. What equipment and supplies do people need to survive these natural disasters?
3. What kind of emergency situation have you experienced in your life?
4. What happens when people panic in emergency situations?
5. What kind of preparation helps people to be ready to evacuate their homes?
6. What's the best way to cope with a medical emergency such as a heart attack?

Grammar: Unreal conditional in the present

Unreal conditional in the present	
Condition	**Result**
if + subject + simple past verb	subject + *would* + base form of verb
If they had more time,	they **would** read more books.

*We use the unreal conditional to imagine a situation that is not true.
*When the verb *be* is in the *if* clause, we always use *were*. (*Was* is only used informally.)
   If I **were** you, I would not lend him any money.
*The *if* clause can come before or after the result clause.
   He would play the guitar better **if** he practiced more.

A. Match the conditions to the results.

1. If you fell from a high place, ___
2. If you planned for emergencies, ___
3. You would die of thirst ___
4. If you had a serious illness, ___
5. You would be electrocuted ___

a. a doctor would diagnose it.
b. if you were struck by lightning.
c. you would be better prepared.
d. you would probably break your leg.
e. if you were in the desert with no water.

 B. What would you do? Complete the sentences and then compare your ideas with your partner's ideas.

1. If I were bitten by a poisonous snake, I would _____
2. If this building were on fire, I would _____
3. If I were in a flood, I would _____
4. If I felt an earthquake happening, I would _____
5. If I had to buy supplies for a camping trip, I would _____

Conversation

 A. Close your book and listen to the conversation. What advice does Nathan give Isabel?

Track 1-19

Isabel: Nathan, do you ever get worried?
Nathan: About what?
Isabel: Oh, you know—about things that can kill you.
Nathan: Sometimes I think about how we would get out of this apartment building if there were a fire.
Isabel: Right! Or what you would do if you were lost in the mountains after a plane crash!
Nathan: Well, that doesn't sound very likely.
Isabel: That's true, and I hope it never happens, but what if it did happen?
Nathan: Look, you can't worry about everything, but you can prepare for some things.
Isabel: Which things?
Nathan: Things that are more likely to happen, like fires or earthquakes.
Isabel: Good idea. Let's start by making an evacuation plan in case we need to get out of this building.

 B. Practice the conversation with a partner. Then switch roles and practice it again.

 C. Make new conversations about the things you worry about.

✓ **Goal 1**   **Talk about emergency situations**

Talk with a partner about emergency situations that are likely to happen where you live. What would you do in these situations?

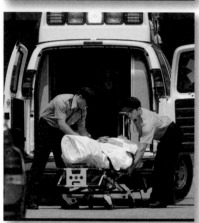

Listening

 A. Listen to a radio call-in show. What situations did the callers survive?

Track 1-20
Caller #1: _____

Caller #2: _____

Caller #3: _____

 B. Listen again. Circle the answers.

Track 1-20
1. When was Caller #1 in an emergency situation?
   a. last week   b. last month   c. last year

2. Where was Caller #2 when his emergency occurred?
   a. at home   b. at work   c. at school

3. What was the result of Caller #3's emergency?
   a. cuts and bruises   b. serious injuries   c. a large payment

Pronunciation: Reduced speech: *D'ya* and *didja*

When people speak quickly, they sometimes shorten or reduce words. For example:

Do you → *D'ya*   Did you → *Didja*

A. Listen and repeat.

Track 1-21

Full form	Reduced speech
1. Do you know the answer?	1. *D'ya* know the answer?
2. Did you get the message?	2. *Didja* get the message?
3. Do you have a plan?	3. *D'ya* have a plan?
4. Did you take an aspirin?	4. *Didja* take an aspirin?

 B. Listen to the questions and circle the form you hear.

Track 1-22
1.   full   reduced
2.   full   reduced
3.   full   reduced
4.   full   reduced
5.   full   reduced
6.   full   reduced

C. Write two questions with *Do you . . .?* and two with *Did you . . .?* Then ask a partner your questions using reduced speech.

Engage!

Did the callers on the radio show do the right thing? Is there anything you would do differently in those situations?

Communication

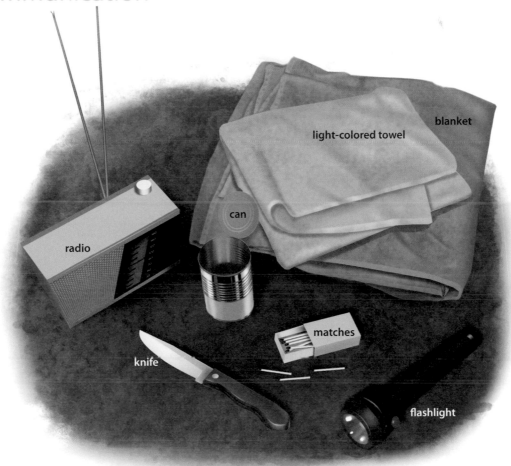

 A. Discuss with a partner how each of these items could help you survive in an emergency. Then choose the three you think would be the most useful.

a blanket	a plastic trash bag	an empty can	matches
water	a cell phone	snack foods	a flashlight
a knife	a radio	a first-aid kit	a light-colored towel

 B. Get together with another pair of students and compare the items you chose. Try to agree on the three most useful survival tools.

✓ **Goal 2**   **Evaluate survival methods**

Tell a partner about a particular situation in which the tools you chose in exercise **A** would be very important. Say how they would help the situation.

Language Expansion: Environmental conservation

A. Read the article. Notice the words in **blue**.

New Zealand Coastal Reserves

When it comes to survival, animals and plants sometimes face as many challenges as people. So New Zealand is doing something to protect its ocean **species**. The country has **banned** all types of fishing in 31 ocean reserves—areas devoted to the **preservation** of marine life.

When the first reserve was opened in 1977, many residents in the area were opposed to the idea. But when the fishing stopped, the **ecosystem** in Goat Island Bay recovered quickly. The snapper returned to the area, and these **predatory** fish began to eat the sea urchins that had destroyed many ocean plants. As the ocean habitat was **restored**, **endangered** species increased in number.

Surprisingly, New Zealand's coastal reserves have also helped the fishing industry. Fish eggs and baby fish drift outside the reserves, replenishing the surrounding areas. Today, commercial fishermen are some of the strongest defenders of the reserves.

● Marine reserve
0 mi   100
0 km   100
NGM MAPS

▲ marine reserve areas in New Zealand

B. Fill in each blank with one of the words in **blue**.

1. Parts of the ocean where you can't go fishing are called _____.
2. _____ animals eat other animals.
3. When something is _____, it goes back to the way it was before.
4. A _____ is a certain kind of plant or animal.
5. When something is _____, it is prohibited by law.
6. _____ means keeping or maintaining something.
7. An _____ is all the plants and animals in a certain area.
8. An _____ species is one that might become extinct soon.

Grammar: *Wish* in the present

A. Read these sentences and answer the questions *Yes* or *No*.

I wish my country had coastal reserves.
1. Does the speaker's country have coastal reserves? _____

I wish I could talk to the president about it.
2. Can the speaker talk to the president? _____

I wish today were Saturday so that I could go to the beach.
3. Is today Saturday? _____

Engage!

Do you think fishing or hunting should be banned where you live? What other ways can you think of to preserve plant and animal species?

Wish in the present

*We use *wish* when we want things to be different than they really are.
  I **wish** I didn't have to get up early. (In reality, I do have to get up early.)

*The verb or auxiliary after *wish* changes in tense, going "backward" in time:

simple present → simple past present continuous → past continuous can →could	I **wish** I **had** a lot of money. I **wish** the fish **were being** protected. I **wish** I **could** speak Russian.	(I don't have a lot of money.) (The fish are not being protected.) (I can't speak Russian.)

B. Fill in each blank with the correct form of the word in parentheses.

1. I wish I _____ (know) the answer, but I'm afraid I can't help you.
2. I wish I _____ (be) eating lunch right now instead of doing this.
3. Akira wishes he _____ (can) drive a car.
4. I wish we _____ (not, have) to take this test.
5. Many people wish they _____ (have) more money.
6. I wish my best friend _____ (be) here. I want to talk to her.

 C. Tell a partner about things you wish were different than they really are. Use all three forms from the chart.

Conversation

 A. Close your book and listen to the conversation. In what ways do meerkats cooperate in order to survive?

Track 1-23

Andrew: Do you ever wish you were an animal?
Caleb: Sure. Sometimes I wish I were a bird so I could fly.
Andrew: I wish I were a meerkat.
Caleb: A meerkat? What's that?
Andrew: It's an African animal. It survives by living in groups and cooperating.
Caleb: How do they cooperate?
Andrew: When there's a predator nearby, they make a warning sound. Then all the meerkats go into their holes.
Caleb: That sounds helpful. What else do they do?
Andrew: They babysit for each other. That way, the parents have a chance to find food.
Caleb: I see what you mean. They're a very social animal.
Andrew: Right, and if I were a meerkat, I wouldn't have to carry these boxes by myself. I could get some help from you!
Caleb: Oh, sorry. Can I give you a hand with those?

Real Language

When you *give someone a hand*, you help them do some work.

 B. Practice the conversation with a partner. Then switch roles and practice it again.

✓ Goal 3　Consider animal survival

Work in a group. Make a list of several animals and discuss some of the things these animals do to survive. Tell your group which animal you wish you were and why.

Reading

 A. What happens at a survival school? Discuss with a partner. List three activities you think you will read about in the article.

_____

_____

_____

 B. Answer the following questions. If necessary look back at the article.

1. Give two reasons people might want to visit southern Utah.
2. When did BOSS start teaching people to survive outdoors?
3. What materials do BOSS students use to make shelters?
4. What materials do BOSS students use to make fire?
5. What kind of people can participate in BOSS courses?
6. What do BOSS students like about survival school?

 C. Tell a partner about the kind of challenges you enjoy. Then talk about a specific experience in your life that has increased your confidence.

 Boulder, Utah, USA

Survival School

Southern Utah in the United States is a land of extremes. The normally dry desert is occasionally drowned in summer rainstorms. The high altitude of Utah's mountains makes the days very hot and the nights very cold. It is also a beautiful place with a long history of human habitation. Utah is named after the Ute tribe of Native Americans, and, before the Ute, the Anasazi people made their home here.

Perhaps it's no surprise that modern outdoor adventurers come to southern Utah to go hiking, camping, and horseback riding in the area's national forests or to see the fantastic rock formations in Bryce Canyon National Park. What might surprise you is that some of the adventurers choose to spend their time outdoors with little food or water and no modern camping equipment. Instead, they're learning to live in the wilderness the old-fashioned way.

The Boulder Outdoor Survival School (BOSS), founded in 1968, is the world's oldest survival school. With its philosophy

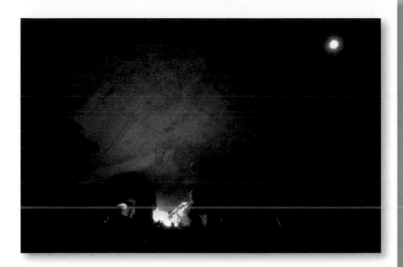

of "Know more; carry less," BOSS teaches its students techniques for surviving outdoors without tents, backpacks, or sleeping bags. Participants learn to make shelters from leaves or snow, to find and **purify** water for drinking, and to eat what they can find in the wild. The students and instructors end their day around a crackling campfire, but the fire is made using stones and **brush** from the area, not matches.

The school's courses are not for everyone. Students must arrive in excellent physical health in order to **endure** hikes of up to 30 miles through Utah's deserts and **canyons**. They must be active learners because they'll need all the skills the BOSS instructors teach them in order to survive a field course, which can last from one week to one month, and which includes "solo" time, when students are tested in a very real way on everything they've learned.

For the people who take BOSS's courses, there is nothing better. If they wanted to spend time outdoors in comfort, they would pack their camping equipment and perhaps their GPS system and join the rest of Utah's outdoor **enthusiasts**. Instead, these campers love the way BOSS challenges their minds and bodies. And the confidence they gain from knowing how to survive without a lot of technology is the reward these brave people are looking for.

Word Focus

purify = to make clean and safe to drink
brush = dry plants and sticks of wood used for burning
endure = to continue with a difficult activity over a long period of time
canyon = a narrow area with steep sides between two mountains
enthusiast = a person who is very interested in an activity or subject

Communication

A. Think of a place in your country where a survival school would work well. Make a list with the name of the place and several reasons why it would be a good place for a survival school. Then list things the students at the school would learn and experience.

B. Get together with another pair of students and compare your lists. Try to agree on which location would be the best for a survival school.

Writing

Choose one of the locations you discussed above and write two paragraphs for an advertising brochure. In the first paragraph, describe the place and explain why it's a good location for the school. In the second paragraph, describe the things students do and learn.

✓ Goal 4   Describe a survival school

Share your two paragraphs with a partner. Tell your partner which parts of his or her writing you like the most. Suggest other details your partner could add.

Before You Watch

A. Chinchero, Peru, is a small village in the Andes Mountains. Underline the ways you think the Chinchero villagers might make their living.

herding animals such as sheep
raising crops such as potatoes
working in big office buildings

selling local crafts to tourists
managing a large discount store
teaching at local schools

B. Work with a partner. List some ways men and women used to make a living and ways they make a living now.

	Men's work	Women's work
In the past		
Now		

While You Watch

A. Watch the video. Circle **T** for *true* and **F** for *false*. Then change the false statements to make them true.

1. Sheep are raised for their wool in Chinchero.   T   F
2. Many of the men in Chinchero are farmers.   T   F
3. Many of the women in Chinchero weave textiles.   T   F
4. Farming is the only way to make money in Chinchero.   T   F
5. Older women teach weaving to younger women.   T   F

B. Watch the video again and take brief notes to answer these questions:

1. How does weaving contribute to economic survival in Chinchero?
2. How does weaving contribute to cultural survival in Chinchero?

C. Watch the video again and circle the correct word.

1. The women in Chinchero manage a weavers' (company/cooperative).
2. Farmers in Chinchero produce very good (barley/tomatoes).
3. Today, farmers don't make enough money to support a (big/whole) family.
4. Nowadays, some of the men help with the (farming/weaving) industry.
5. Young women earn money by selling the blankets and (clothes/hats) they make.

After You Watch

What traditional products are made where you live? Design a tourism brochure with a brief description of these products.

Communication

You are members of the Center for Traditional Textiles cooperative. Brainstorm a list of new ways to market and sell your products.

Center for Traditional Textiles
Uniting farmers and weavers since 1986

1.

2.

3.

4.

5.

ART

1. Which word describes each work of art?
   What do you see in each one?
   a. sculpture
   b. drawing
   c. painting
   d. stained glass

2. Which one do you like the most? Why?

UNIT GOALS

Report what another person said
Express your opinions about a piece of art
Describe your favorite artists and their art
Talk about public art

Vocabulary

A. Read the article. Notice the words in **blue**.

Artist of the Year: Margaret Tafoya

Margaret Tafoya is a Pueblo Indian potter—like all the women in her family. "My daughters are doing work from the same clay that my grandmother used," she said.

The Pueblo **technique** for making pots is unusual. Each pot is made from small strips of clay, and then rubbed with stones until it's perfectly smooth. Pueblo Indian pots always have beautiful shapes, but each artist has an individual **style**. Margaret is famous for making very large pots.

The potters decorate their work by carving **designs** in the wet clay. Margaret uses **abstract** designs on her pots, with shapes that **represent** rain clouds, water snakes, and other things that are important in her culture. She said, "We do it so that we will remember." Other Pueblo Indian potters use more realistic pictures such as bear footprints. All of these designs **express** the Pueblo Indians' closeness to the world of nature.

B. Write the words in **blue** next to their meanings.

1. show what you think or feel about something _____
2. a pattern of lines or shapes that is used to decorate something _____
3. a way of making art that is used by one artist, or a small group _____
4. a particular way to do or make something _____
5. to be a symbol for something _____
6. describes art made with shapes and lines, not pictures of real things _____

C. Talk about these pieces using the vocabulary from exercise **A**. Then guess which country each one is from.

Morocco China Netherlands

Grammar: Reported speech: Statements

Quoted speech	Reported speech
"I'm an artist."	Margaret said (that) she was an artist.
"I won an award."	She said she had won an award.
"We do it so that we will remember."	Margaret said they did it so that they would remember.

> * In reported speech, we tell what another person said. The word *that* is optional.
> * The verb usually changes to a different (past) tense.
> "I **paint** every day." He said he **painted** every day. "Janie **went** home." He said Janie **had gone** home.
> * The pronouns also change.
> "**I'm** tired and **my** head hurts." She said **she** was tired and **her** head hurt.
> * Some other words change too.
> "Frank isn't **here**." He said Frank wasn't **there**. "I'll come back **tomorrow**." She said she would come back **the next day**.

A. Andy Chao has won an award as Young Artist of the Year. Read what he said in the interview and write his statements in reported speech.

1. "I make sculptures with glass and metal." He said he _____
2. "My newest sculpture is 10 meters tall." _____
3. "I'm flying to Germany tomorrow." _____
4. "I don't know how long I'll stay in Berlin." _____
5. "I'm going to show my work in a famous gallery." _____
6. "I can't talk about my next sculpture." _____

> Carmen said she was having a very bad day.

> Really? What happened?

 B. Think about the last time you talked to your best friend on the phone. Use reported speech to tell your partner about the conversation.

Conversation

 A. Listen to the conversation with your book closed. What did Jennie's brother say about the paintings?

Track 1-24

Mia: Hi, Jennie. What did you do over the weekend?
Jennie: Nothing special on Saturday, but on Sunday I went to the student painting show at the art institute.
Mia: You're kidding! I thought you didn't like art very much.
Jennie: Well, I don't usually, but my brother told me about it. He said the paintings were amazing.
Mia: So, what did you think of them?
Jennie: I thought they were great! A lot of them were realistic, with the most wonderful details.
Mia: There are some really talented painters there.
Jennie: Yeah, you're right. Of course, some of the other paintings were kind of strange. One of them was just three blue circles.

 B. Practice the conversation with a partner. Then make new conversations about these pictures.

Real Language

You're kidding! is an informal expression that shows you're surprised or don't believe what the other person said.

▲ sculpture garden

▲ stained glass exhibit

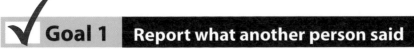

✓ Goal 1 Report what another person said

What did your partner say about the photos in exercise **B**? Tell a new partner.

Listening

👥 **A.** Look at these paintings. Describe them to a partner.

a.

b.

c.

d.

e.

> Painting A is abstract, but I think it represents feelings.

Engage!

Which of the paintings do you like the most? Why?

🎧 Track 1-25

B. You are going to hear conversations in a museum about three of these paintings. Write the letter of the painting the people are talking about.

Conversation 1: ___   Conversation 2: ___   Conversation 3: ___

🎧 Track 1-25

C. Listen to the conversations again. What does the man think about each painting?

Conversation 1: It's (boring/peaceful/exciting).
Conversation 2: It's (colorful/dramatic/realistic).
Conversation 3: It's (happy/little/relaxing).

👥 **D.** Do you agree with the man's ideas about the paintings? Explain your answers to a partner.

Pronunciation: Quoted and indirect speech

A. Listen to the difference in these sentences. Notice the pause before the quotation marks and the stronger voice in quoted speech.

Track 1-26

She said, "It was important."　　　　She said it was important.
"Who?" said Alexander.　　　　　　Who said "Alexander?"

B. Listen and circle the letter of the sentence you hear.

Track 1-27

1. a. Mark said he didn't know.　　　　b. Mark said, "He didn't know."
2. a. John said it was a nice painting.　　b. John said, "It was a nice painting."
3. a. I said I couldn't help him.　　　　b. I said, "I couldn't help him."
4. a. Bella says she's an artist.　　　　b. Bella says, "She's an artist."
5. a. She said she had some money.　　b. She said, "She had some money."
6. a. He said they went home.　　　　b. He said, "They went home."

C. Practice reading the sentences in exercise **B** with a partner.

Communication

A. Discuss the paintings on the previous page and pick the best one to hang in each of these places. Choose a different painting for each place.

- a very expensive restaurant
- the waiting room in a hospital
- the living room of a family apartment
- the office of a company president

B. Explain your decisions to the class.

Goal 2　**Express your opinion about a piece of art**

Which of the paintings do you like the least? Explain your opinion to a partner.

Language Expansion: Materials

A. Read the advertisement.

> **Come to the Korean Folk Village, south of Seoul!**
>
> Here, you can meet people who make traditional crafts. You'll find presents that are perfect for all your friends. We have **clay** pottery and beautiful **leather** bags. Try on a pair of sandals made of **straw** or a **wood** mask used in old dances. **Bamboo** crafts like boxes and baskets are famous in Korea. Korea also has great artists who make things with metal like **gold** necklaces and **brass** bowls. You can even take home a **stone** statue!

B. Label the photos with the words in **blue** from exercise **A**.

1. _____

2. _____

3. _____

4. _____

5. _____

6. _____

7. _____

8. _____

> My city is famous for animal masks. They're made of paper.

C. What are some traditional crafts from your country? What are they made of?

Grammar: Subject adjective clauses

Statements	Adjective clause
You can meet <u>people</u>. (<u>They</u> make traditional crafts.)	You can meet people **who make traditional crafts**.
You'll find <u>presents</u>. (<u>They</u> are perfect for all your friends.)	You'll find **presents that are perfect for all your friends**.
An <u>artist</u> has strong hands. (<u>He</u> works with clay.)	An artist **who works with clay has strong hands**

* An adjective clause modifies (gives more information about) a noun. It comes after the noun.
* Use *who* in adjective clauses about people, to replace *he*, *she*, or *they*.
* Use *that* in adjective clauses about things, to replace *it* or *they*. We can use *which* instead of *that* in more formal sentences.

A. Write sentences with adjective clauses about these artists' work. Use the information in the box.

~~paint pictures~~   write books   make movies   write poems   carve statues   write pop songs

1. A painter _is a person who paints pictures._
2. A poet _____
3. A songwriter _____
4. A sculptor _____
5. An author _____
6. A director _____

B. Write sentences with subject adjective clauses that modify the underlined word.

1. I bought a <u>pot</u>. It was made in Korea.   _I bought a pot that was made in Korea._
2. Jenna has two <u>brothers</u>. They are artists. _____
3. The <u>woman</u> is from Brazil. She lives next door. _____
4. <u>Everyone</u> learned a lot. They took the class. _____
5. Where is the <u>book</u>? It was on the table. _____
6. I don't like those <u>paintings</u>. They are hard to understand. _____

Conversation

A. Listen to the conversation with your book closed. What kind of crafts does Carrie like?

Track 1-28

Emily: Where did you get that jacket, Carrie? It's really beautiful!

Carrie: Thank you! I bought it in the Fair Trade store. They have crafts from all different countries, and they pay the artists a fair price.

Emily: Sounds interesting. What else do they have there?

Carrie: Oh, lots of cool things! I also bought some coffee cups from Mexico, and I've been using them every day. I really like crafts that are useful.

Emily: Do you? For me, the most important thing is the style. I want crafts that look handmade—not like they came from a machine.

Carrie: Well, I'm sure you can find something you like there.

Emily: Next time you go, I'd like to go along.

> **Real Language**
>
> When someone says something nice about us, we say, *thank you*.

 B. Practice the conversation. Then make new conversations about these things. Use your own opinions.

> I like clothes that don't cost much!

    paintings   cooking utensils   clothes

✓ Goal 3   Describe your favorite artists and their art

Work with a partner. Take turns describing your favorite artists and their creations. Use subject adjective clauses in your descriptions.

Reading

A. List all of the places where you can see art in your city. What can you see in each place?

 B. Match the sentence parts to show the reasons.

1. Artists didn't maintain their murals ___.
2. The government painted over some murals ___.
3. The murals are in bad condition ___.
4. Artists in L.A. started painting murals ___.
5. The government is spending $1.7 million ___.
6. Artists like murals ___.

a. because of dirty air and hot weather
b. because it was difficult and dangerous
c. because so many people see them
d. to cover up graffiti
e. to save murals in Los Angeles
f. because they liked the work of Mexican artists

 **C.** Discuss these questions with a partner.

1. Describe the murals in the pictures. What do you think they represent?
2. What is your opinion of these murals? Explain your reasons.
3. Would murals like this be popular in your city? Why, or why not?

People like art that makes them smile!

Word Focus

mural = a painting that is made on a wall
graffiti = words that are written on a wall in a public place
diversity = including many different types of people

 Los Angeles, California, USA

Saving a City's Public Art

Avoiding L.A.'s traffic jams may be impossible, but the city's colorful freeway **murals** can brighten even the worst commute. Paintings that depict famous people and historical scenes cover office buildings and freeway walls all across the city. With a collection of more than 2,000 murals, Los Angeles is the unofficial mural capital of the world.

But the combination of **graffiti**, pollution, and hot sun has left many L.A. murals in terrible condition. The city, trying to stop the spread of graffiti, has painted over some of the murals completely. In the past, experts say, little attention was given to caring for public art. Artists were even expected to maintain their own works, not an easy task with cars racing by along the freeway.

Now the city is beginning a huge project to restore the city's murals. The work started in 2003. So far, 16 walls have been selected, and more may be added later.

Until about 1960, public murals in Los Angeles were rare. But in the '60s and '70s, young L.A. artists began to study early 20th-century Mexican mural painting. Soon, their murals became a symbol of the city's cultural expression and a showcase for L.A.'s cultural **diversity**.

The most famous mural in the city is Judith Baca's "The Great Wall," a 13-foot-high (4-meter-high) painting that runs for half a mile (0.8 kilometer) in North Hollywood. The mural represents the history of **ethnic** groups in California. It took eight years to complete—400 **underprivileged** teenagers painted the designs—and is probably the longest mural in the world.

One of the murals that will be restored now is Kent Twitchell's "Seventh Street Altarpiece," which he painted for the Los Angeles Olympics in 1984. This striking work **depicts** two people facing each other on opposite sides of the freeway near downtown Los Angeles. "It was meant as a kind of gateway through which the traveler to L.A. must drive," said Twitchell. "The open hands represent peace."

Artists often call murals *the people's art.* Along a busy freeway or hidden in a quiet neighborhood, murals can reach people who would never pay money to see fine art in a museum. "Murals give a voice to the silent **majority**," said one artist.

Communication

 A. Your group is in charge of planning a new piece of public art for the area near your school.

1. What kind of art will you have? A mural, sculpture, stained glass, or something else?
2. Where will the art be located?
3. Draw a picture of the art.

B. Present your group's ideas to the class.

Writing

Write about a work of art that you like. Describe what it looks like and what it represents and explain why you like it.

✓ **Goal 4** **Talk about public art**

Describe a piece of public art that you like (or don't like).

Before You Watch

A. Discuss the questions with a partner.

1. What is the oldest kind of art in your country? Where can you see it today?
2. Do people still make this kind of art in your country?

B. Read the information and study the words in **bold.**

Aboriginal people lived in Australia before the first settlers came from Europe. Their **civilization** is the oldest on earth. Before they had writing, they used art to keep a **primitive** record of their history. They used a kind of soil called **ochre** to paint on rock. Groups of families called **clans** painted different kinds of pictures to tell about the *dreamtime* at the beginning of the world.

While You Watch

A. Watch the video and write down words that describe the aboriginal paintings. Then compare your answers with a partner.

_____

_____

B. Watch the video again. Circle **T** for *true* and **F** for *false*.

1. Aboriginal artists were painting before people from Europe came to Australia.	T	F
2. Many of the rock paintings are in a national park.	T	F
3. Aboriginal people came to Australia 4,000 years ago.	T	F
4. Some aboriginal paintings tell about things from everyday life.	T	F
5. Each artist could paint many different kinds of animals.	T	F
6. The old rock paintings are in very good condition now.	T	F

 C. Watch the video again. Check the things that are the same now as in the past and the things that are different.

	the same	different
1. the colors that artists paint with		
2. the things that artists paint on		
3. the designs that artists use		
4. the prices of the paintings		
5. the condition of old paintings		

After You Watch

 Discuss the questions with a partner.

1. Why do people want to buy aboriginal paintings?
2. Would you like to have an aboriginal painting in your house? Explain your reasons.

Communication

1. Think about an important time in your life and draw a "rock painting" about it. Use simple pictures and symbols.
 2. Get together with a group. Take turns showing your "rock paintings." Ask and answer questions about their meanings.

GETTING AROUND

1. Which form of transportation is the most important in your country now?
   a. rail
   b. air
   c. water
   d. motor vehicle

2. Which will be the most important in the future?

UNIT GOALS

Talk about new developments in transportation

Talk about choices in transportation

Use English to get around

Make recommendations for improving transportation

UNIT 7

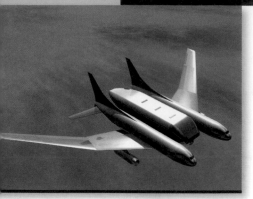

Vocabulary

 A. Read the article. Which of these ideas do you think will be successful?

The Future of Flying

- Today, the largest airplanes carry up to 600 **passengers**, but the size of planes will **increase**. New airplanes have been designed that will carry up to 900 people.
- You won't need to stop and change planes during a trip. Very small jets called "Personal Air Vehicles" will take people **directly** to their **destinations**.
- Many modern airplanes are flown by computers between the take-off and the landing. In the future some planes won't have a **pilot** at all.
- There are plans for huge **freight** planes that will be 100 meters long and fly across the ocean only 7 meters above the water, at a low **speed**.
- Quieter and more **efficient** planes are being developed. New materials and designs will **reduce** their use of **fuel**.

B. Write the words in **blue** next to their meanings.

1. places you are going to _____
2. to become greater in number or amount _____
3. how fast something moves _____
4. without stopping or changing direction _____
5. a substance like gasoline or oil that is burned to give power _____
6. things that are transported on a vehicle _____
7. to make smaller _____
8. a person who is trained to fly an airplane _____
9. not using too much time or energy _____
10. people who are traveling in a vehicle _____

Grammar: Passive voice with present continuous and present perfect tenses

Passive voice with present continuous tense *am/is/are* + *being* + past participle	Passive voice with present perfect tense *have/has* + *been* + past participle
More efficient planes **are being developed**.	New types of planes **have been designed**.

* The passive voice can be used with any tense.

* Use the passive voice with the present continuous tense to talk about things that are in progress now.

    *The new plane **is being tested** now.*

* Use the passive voice with the present perfect tense to talk about things in the past that have an effect in the present.

    *Computers **have been used** for more than 50 years.*

A. Complete the article with the passive present continuous tense of the verbs in parentheses.

Cars for Tomorrow

New discoveries _are being made_ (make) every day. Automobiles are changing very fast. Already, energy-efficient cars _____ (sell) in many countries. Very small, light cars for one person _____ (design). Cars that run on hydrogen _____ (test), and electric vehicles _____ (use) in some cities. More corn _____ (grow) to make ethanol for fuel.

B. Complete the sentences with the passive present perfect form of a verb from the box.

spend	repair	find	make	design	sell

1. The government admitted that mistakes _have been made_ .
2. A lot of money _____ to solve our city's transportation problems.
3. Cars _____ that burn wood, but they are very slow and dirty.
4. My computer _____ four times now. I think I need a new one!
5. Did you hear the news? The lost children _____ .
6. Thousands of gas-electric hybrid cars _____ in the last five years.

Conversation

Track 2-2

A. Listen to the conversation with your book closed. What kind of car will the man get next month?

Cassie: The price of gas is getting so high. I think I'm going to get rid of my car and take the bus.

Jake: Not me! I'm getting a new car next month. It's a hybrid.

Cassie: You mean one of those electric cars?

Jake: Not exactly. It uses both electricity and gasoline.

Cassie: Well, I don't like to be the first person to try something new. New technology always has a lot of problems.

Jake: That's not always true. Besides, electric cars have been used for a long time.

Cassie: Well, I'd like to see your hybrid car when you get it. Will you take me for a ride?

Jake: Sure! And maybe I'll even let you drive it.

B. Practice the conversation. Then talk about these new kinds of cars.

 **Goal 1** **Talk about new developments in transportation**

Tell a partner about a new way of getting around in your country.

Listening

 A. Discuss these questions with a partner.

1. What are some famous cities with subways? Have you ever used a subway?
2. What are some advantages and disadvantages of subways?

Track 2-3

B. You are going to hear a radio program about things from the past that were discovered while building subways. Number the pictures in the order that you hear about them.

▲ stone wall   ▲ fossil   ▲ pyramid

Track 2-3

C. Listen to the radio program again and write the information.

1. City: _____
   Year of discovery: _____
   They decided to _____
2. City: _____
   Year of discovery: _____
   They decided to _____
3. City: _____
   Year of discovery: _____
   They decided to _____

 D. Are there any disagreements about transportation in your city or country? What's your opinion?

> I don't think a new highway is a good idea because . . .

Pronunciation: Reduced *are*

Track 2-4

A. The word *are* sounds like /r/ in the middle of a sentence. Notice the pronunciation of *are* in these sentences.

The buses **are** crowded.   Cars **are** parked on the street.

B. Read these sentences, paying attention to the pronunciation of *are*.

1. Those books are really funny.
2. How much are the tickets?
3. Those computers are made in China.
4. People are talking about him.
5. Cheaper cars are being sold.
6. Where are my keys?

Communication

A. Read the situation.

Lomeria is a large city in a developing country. The airport in Lomeria is 50 years old and too small for the newest airplanes. Because of this, Lomeria is building a new airport. Now the terminal is being built. Last week, workers at the construction site uncovered an ancient city from 2,000 years ago, and construction has stopped until the city government decides what to do. Many people have very strong opinions about the subject. People in the neighborhood don't want a new airport, because they say it will cause noise and pollution. Other people in the city say that the airport is needed for the tourists who come to Lomeria to experience its history and culture.

B. You are members of the Lomeria city council. Role-play a meeting about the airport problem. Read the possible plans, and add one more idea. Then discuss the plans and decide which one is the best.

Plan 1: Continue building the new airport. Don't change the plan.
Plan 2: Change the plan. Build a smaller airport in the same place, and preserve one part of the ancient city.
Plan 3: Stop construction of the new airport, and use the money to preserve the ancient city.
Plan 4: Stop construction. Try to get more money to build a new airport in a different place.
Plan 5: Move the ancient city to a new place, and then finish building the airport.
Plan 6: _____

✔ **Goal 2**   **Talk about choices in transportation**

Explain your decision to the class.

Language Expansion: Public transportation

A. Read the article and label the pictures with the words in **blue**.

Buses for the Future

The city of Curitiba, Brazil, has the most convenient and modern bus system in the world, called Bus Rapid Transit. Very large buses for up to 300 people travel on major roads all around the city. Passengers **board** the buses from comfortable glass *tube stations*. If they don't have a **pass** or a **ticket**, they pay their **fare** in the station, so everyone gets on the bus very quickly when it arrives. They can **transfer** to another **route** without paying again. Where different bus routes connect, there are comfortable **terminals**, with telephones, small shops, and rest rooms. The system is very fast and efficient, and it's very popular with the people of Curitiba. More than 70 percent of the commuters there travel by bus every day.

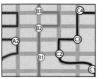     

1. _____ 2. _____ 3. _____ 4. _____ 5. _____ 6. _____ 7. _____

B. Discuss the questions with a partner.

1. What kind of public transportation does your city have? Do you like to use it? Why, or why not?
2. Do you think Bus Rapid Transit would work well in your city? Explain your reasons.

Grammar: Indirect questions

Question	Polite phrase +	indirect question
Where is the bus stop?	Do you know	**where** the bus stop is?
How much do the tickets cost?	Could you please tell me	**how much** the tickets cost?
Is the train on time?	Can you tell me	**whether/if** the train is on time?
Do I need a reservation?	I'd like to know	**whether/if** I need a reservation.

* An indirect question is a question that's placed inside another question or statement. We often use indirect questions in polite speech.
* In an indirect *wh-* question, the subject comes before the verb.
* In an indirect *yes/no* question, use *whether* (more formal) or *if* (less formal) in the question.
* Don't use the auxiliary *do/does* in indirect questions.

A. Write polite indirect questions.

1. Does this train go to Central Station? (do you know) _____

   _____

2. What time does the movie start? (can you tell me) _____

3. Is there a subway station near here? (could you please tell me) _____

   _____

4. When is our next test? (I'd like to know) _____

   _____

5. Where's the bathroom? (can you tell me) _____

   _____

 B. Choose a famous person and role-play a newspaper reporter interviewing this person. The reporter should ask polite indirect questions to get as much information as possible about the items in the box. Then change roles and practice again.

| age | marital status | hometown | work | hobbies | future plans |

> Do you know when you'll make your next movie?

Conversation

 A. Luis is in a subway station in Tokyo. Listen to the conversation with your book closed. Where does he want to go?

Track 2-5

Luis: Excuse me. Do you speak English?

Yuki: Yes, a little.

Luis: Could you please tell me how to get to the Imperial Palace Garden?

Yuki: From here, you take the Tozai subway line to Hibiya Station. Then you walk for about five minutes.

Luis: And can you tell me where I can buy a ticket?

Yuki: You get them from that machine. Let's see . . . the fare is 250 yen. You put your money in here and push this button.

Luis: Great! Oh, one more question—do you know where I board the train?

Yuki: Just go down those stairs and you'll see a sign that says Tozai Line. It's in English.

Luis: Thanks for your help!

Yuki: You're welcome.

Real Language

When we want to stop a person on the street to ask a question, we say *Excuse me.*

 B. Practice the conversation.

✓ **Goal 3** **Use English to get around**

> You take bus number 7 to the university, and then transfer to . . .

Make new conversations with a partner about how to get to places in your city.

Reading

 A. Discuss the questions with a partner.

1. What kinds of transportation did your city have 50 years ago?
2. Are those kinds of transportation still used today? Why, or why not?

Word Focus

migrant = person who moves regularly for work

poverty = the condition of being poor

at a stretch = at one time, without stopping

authorities = people in important positions

congestion = the condition of being crowded

crawl = move along very slowly

B. Circle **T** for *true* and **F** for *false*. Correct the false statements.

1. Rickshaws are a traditional form of transportation in Kolkata.   T   F
2. The men who pull the rickshaws earn a lot of money.   T   F
3. Rickshaws can be used in parts of the city where buses can't drive.   T   F
4. Rickshaws are mostly used by wealthy people.   T   F
5. Rickshaws are a problem in heavy traffic.   T   F
6. The government is trying to increase the number of rickshaws.   T   F
7. There are programs now to help the rickshaw pullers get new jobs.   T   F

Kolkata, India

The Rickshaws of Kolkata

Hand-pulled rickshaws first appeared in Kolkata, India, a century ago, and about 6,000 of them still roll through the streets today. Most men who pull them are poor, aging **migrants** from the countryside. Their vehicles are not being made any more, and as the parts wear out, they cannot be replaced. Thus, the rickshaw is nearing its end in Kolkata.

Rickshaws are an important form of transportation in this city of nearly 15 million people. They are cheap and convenient. Poor and middle-class residents rely on rickshaws to move through narrow lanes in areas of the central city not served by public transportation. Families often pay a rickshaw to take their children to and from school.

Rickshaws also provide delivery service for hotels, shops, and homes around the city, carting everything from food for 500 wedding guests to live chickens. Ladies on shopping trips depend on rickshaws to wait while they make several stops before returning home. Some people even use a rickshaw instead of an ambulance.

But rickshaw pullers live in extreme **poverty**. Most of them are homeless. Some sleep in a *dera*, a rickshaw garage; others simply live in their rickshaws or on the street. They work for more than 12 hours **at a stretch**, earning about 100 rupees ($2.50) a day. Their top priority is paying the rent on their vehicles, then buying food and shelter. They also have to bribe the city police who enforce rickshaw laws. Any extra money goes to their families back home.

For the last 10 years, the government has been trying to get rid of the rickshaws. City **authorities** say they want to modernize Kolkata's image. They also want to reduce traffic congestion: "We must be fair to the cars and buses that are **crawling** because of the rickshaws," one city official said.

What will the rickshaw pullers do for work in the future? Most are 40 to 60 years old and have no job skills. Local authorities have talked about programs to retrain the pullers. They could drive auto-rickshaws, work in parking lots, or make traditional crafts. However, nothing has been done to start these programs, and rickshaw pullers are understandably very worried about their future. "I'll try anything, even learning a new job, if it will help my family," one puller said.

C. Who would say this? More than one answer may be correct.

	A rick-shaw puller	A wealthy man	A poor woman	A city official
1. Rickshaws are useful transportation for ordinary people.				
2. A car is much better than a rickshaw.				
3. Many people will lose their jobs if there are no rickshaws.				
4. Rickshaws are good for Kolkata because they are cheap.				
5. Rickshaw pullers need to get new jobs.				
6. A modern city needs faster transportation.				

Communication

What should the city of Kolkata do about the rickshaw problem? Make a list of recommendations for its city government.

Writing

How would you improve the transportation system in your city? Write a letter to the editor of a newspaper explaining your ideas. Begin your letter "Dear Editor." End it with "Sincerely," and sign your name.

 **Goal 4** **Make recommendations for improving transportation**

Tell the class about your recommendations.

Before You Watch

A. Discuss the questions with a partner.

1. How many kinds of transportation can people use to get across your city?
2. Rank them from fastest to slowest.
3. Are your answers for question **2** different for daytime and nighttime?

B. Match the words with their meanings. Use your dictionary if necessary.

1. messenger ___
2. dispatcher ___
3. on commission ___
4. speed ___
5. utmost ___

a. going fast
b. getting paid a percentage of the money you make for your company
c. highest
d. a person who delivers papers and messages
e. a person who sends other people to do things

While You Watch

A. Watch the video and complete the summary.

Video Summary

Every day, in the city of _____, thousands of documents and packages are delivered by people riding _____. Their work is dangerous because they must ride very _____ in heavy traffic. Even though it's difficult, most messengers _____ their work.

B. Watch the video again and write the information.

1. one reason why bicycle messengers like their job: _____
   _____

2. one reason why police officers get angry at messengers: _____
   _____

3. one reason why people in New York dislike bicycle messengers: _____
   _____

4. one reason why bicycle messengers don't like people in cars: _____
   _____

 C. Watch the video a third time and complete the sentences.

1. Every day, in New York City, millions of people crowd the streets, along with more than _____ cars.
2. The messengers race through _____, any way they can.
3. My comment is that they're dangerous. They can _____ you.
4. This company calls for a messenger _____ to _____ times a day.
5. Their work keeps the _____ of New York moving.

After You Watch

 What could be done to make bicycle messengers' jobs safer? With your group, list as many ideas as you can. Then share your ideas with the class.

Communication

Imagine you live in a big city with many bicycle messengers. The city council wants to make a law about bicycle messengers, and it has asked people to give their opinions. Choose one of these roles, and role-play a meeting. With your group, make three recommendations to the city council.

| a bicycle messenger | a police officer | a parent with small children | a business owner |

COMPETITION

1. Which phrase best describes each picture?
   a. winning a race
   b. a boxing match
   c. celebrating as a team
   d. a skiing event

2. Besides sports, what other situations can you think of that involve competition?

UNIT GOALS

Give your opinion about sports

Choose the best sport for your personality type

Talk about positive and negative aspects of competition

Discuss competitive advantages

UNIT 8

Vocabulary

A. Read the sign. Notice the words in **blue.**

> ### Court Rules
>
> - An **athlete** may play in a tennis **match** only with proper **training**. Please make an appointment with an instructor if you need individual help.
> - Players must not **cheat** during a match. Anyone caught cheating will be asked to leave the tennis club.
> - Remember to show good **sportsmanship**. After every match, the **winner** and the **loser** should be polite and shake hands.
> - Doubles players are part of one **team**. You and your tennis partner must sign up in the office before every match.

B. Complete each sentence with one of the words in **blue.**

1. Another word for a player is an _____.
2. A group of people who play together is a _____.
3. To play a sport well, you need a lot of _____.
4. Polite behavior during a sports event is called _____.
5. The person or team that wins is the _____.
6. The person or team that loses is the _____.
7. Some people _____ while playing sports, which means they don't follow the rules.
8. Another word for a game is a _____.

Word Focus

We almost never use the word *sportsmanship* by itself. We talk about *good sportsmanship* or *poor sportsmanship*.

Grammar: Negative questions

Negative questions	Speaker's expectation or attitude
Don't you want to go downtown with us? **Aren't** you happy about winning?	The speaker may expect you to say *yes*. The speaker may be surprised because you don't seem happy.

* Unlike regular *yes/no* questions, negative questions begin with *don't/doesn't* or *aren't/isn't*.
* We can use negative questions to show that we expect a certain answer or to show attitudes such as surprise or annoyance.
* We can answer negative questions in the same way as regular questions.
   Q: Aren't you early?
   A: *Yes, I am.* (if you're early)/*No, I'm not.* (if you're not early)
* Negative questions can also begin with the negative form of a modal, for example, *won't*, *can't*, *shouldn't*, or *wouldn't*.
   Shouldn't you call your parents?   **Won't** they be worried?

A. Read each situation and circle the correct choice.

1. Your friend offers you an orange.
    You: No, thank you.
    Your friend: Oh, don't you like oranges?
    Your friend is probably (surprised/angry).

2. A student gives an assignment to his teacher.
    Teacher: Wasn't this due yesterday?
    Student: Yes, it was. I'm sorry it's late.
    The teacher is probably (happy/annoyed).

3. You and a friend are talking about last week's soccer match.
    You: Now the team might not be in the World Cup.
    Your friend: But, didn't they win last week's match?
    Your friend thinks the team (did/did not) win last week's match.

4. You arrive home after a long bus trip and you look tired.
    Your mother: Aren't you glad to be home?
    Your mother expects you to say (*yes/no*).

B. Work with a partner. Think of a possible situation for each of these negative questions. Imagine and practice the conversations.

- Don't you have any money?
- Isn't your sister a swimmer?
- Aren't these your glasses?
- Doesn't the match start at two thirty?
- Aren't you cold?
- Don't you need this?

Conversation

Track 2-6

A. Listen to the conversation with your book closed. How many different sports do the speakers mention?

Nora: Do you want to go to the game with me tonight?
Stacy: Thanks, but I don't really like watching sports.
Nora: You don't like watching sports? How about playing sports?
Stacy: I like to play badminton, and sometimes I go for a run.
Nora: That's so funny! I only like watching badminton.
Stacy: So which sports do you like to play?
Nora: Basketball is my favorite, but I like to play golf, too.
Stacy: I forgot about basketball! That's a sport I do enjoy watching.

B. Practice the conversation with a partner. Switch roles and practice it again.

✓ **Goal 1**   **Give your opinion about sports**

Make new conversations about sports. Tell your partner which sports you do and don't like.

 Tae kwon do is a popular martial art.

 soccer players

Listening

 A. Work with a partner. Write each sport in the correct place in the diagram.

baseball	soccer	badminton	tennis	skiing	martial arts
swimming	bicycling	volleyball	boxing	basketball	golf

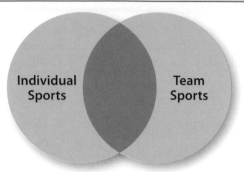

Individual Sports

Team Sports

 B. Discuss these questions with a partner. Give reasons for your answers.

1. What type of person enjoys playing individual sports?
2. What type of person enjoys playing team sports?

C. Listen to three people talking. Decide which sport would be better for each person.

Track 2-7

1. Rita should probably play: ___ golf ___ volleyball
2. Chris should probably train for: ___ marathon running
   ___ the soccer team
3. Susan should probably sign up for: ___ martial arts ___ basketball

D. How did you make your choices in exercise **C**? Listen again and take brief notes on what the speakers say.

Track 2-7

E. Discuss the reasons for your choices in exercise **C**. Refer to your notes and try to agree on the best sport for each speaker.

Communication

A. Take turns. Ask a partner these questions about personality types.

1. Are you an introvert (quiet, shy) or extrovert (social)?
2. Are you a perfectionist, or do you need outside pressure to motivate you?
3. Are you very focused when you do something (you forget about everything else), or are you aware of everything going on around you?
4. Do you like vigorous exercise, such as running, or more gentle exercise?
5. Do you like to concentrate on one thing for a long time, or do you prefer shorter activities that are constantly changing?

B. Recommend a sport for your partner to play based on his or her answers.

Real Language

When you *count on someone*, you depend on them to do something that's important to you.

Pronunciation: Intonation to show surprise

Track 2-8

A. We can use rising intonation in statements to show that we're surprised by something we just heard. The rising intonation makes the statements sound like questions. Listen and repeat these sentences.

1. He left this morning?
2. You're eating carrots?

B. Practice the conversation with a partner. Use rising intonation to show surprise in the underlined sentences.

Barb: I just found out that only men competed in the ancient Olympics.

Arturo: Right, and there was a separate running event for women.

Barb: <u>You already knew that?</u> But you've never read a history book!

Arturo: I saw it on TV. I also learned that there was no marathon race back then.

Barb: <u>No marathon race?</u> I thought that was one of the oldest Olympic events.

Arturo: The race is based on a very old story, but it wasn't part of the ancient Olympics.

Barb: Interesting! Well, maybe you didn't know that there were no medals then. The winning athletes only got a crown made from olive leaves.

Arturo: <u>A crown of leaves?</u> That doesn't sound like a great prize.

Barb: True, but the athletes became famous, and they were treated like celebrities.

Arturo: <u>Really?</u> But how did they get famous without TV?

Barb: In ancient Greece they had other ways to learn about things, I guess.

✓ **Goal 2** | **Choose the best sport for your personality type**

Tell the class which sport your partner recommended for you. Explain why the sport is a good match for your personality, or choose a different sport if it's not a good match.

Language Expansion: Sports

A. Write each word below next to the correct meaning.

| points | coach | championship | score | medal | trophy | scoreboard |

1. a large sign that shows the score during a sports event _____
2. someone who trains a person or a sports team _____
3. a prize such as a cup given to the winner of a competition _____
4. the total number of points a player or team receives in a sports event ____
5. a competition to find the best player or team in a sport _____
6. the numbers that are added together to give the score _____
7. a metal disk given as a prize in a sports event _____

B. Take turns. Ask and answer these questions about the picture.

1. What was the final score of the championship game?
2. How many points did the winning team have?
3. What is the team coach wearing?
4. What is every player wearing around his neck?
5. What is the man in the suit presenting to the team?

Grammar: Object adjective clauses

Statement	Adjective clause
He won a **medal**. <u>It</u> was gold.	The medal **that he won** was gold.
I'm in a **league**. <u>It</u> was formed last year.	The league **which I'm in** was formed last year.
We met a **woman**. <u>She</u> lives in Beijing.	The woman **who(m) we met** lives in Beijing.

* An object adjective clause modifies a noun that is the object of a verb or a preposition.
* Use *that* or *which* in object adjective clauses about things.
* Use *whom* in adjective clauses about people, or use *who* in informal speaking.
* The pronoun (*that*, *which*, or *whom*) in an object adjective clause can sometimes be omitted.

Read an excerpt from a blog. Fill in each blank with *that*, *which*, or *whom*. There may be more than one correct answer.

Engage!

Are the lessons that competitive sports teach us helpful or harmful?

⊗ ⊖ ⊕ Blog Entry

File   Edit   View   Help

Subject: Envy between friends

Yesterday I ran into an old friend _____ I hadn't seen in several months. We started chatting, and I told my friend about the new job _____ I got last week. As I described my coworkers, my job duties, and the place where I work, I could see something in my friend's eyes that surprised me. It was envy! Most of the people _____ I had told about my job were happy for me, but this old friend has always been very competitive. She is able to be happy about the good things that happen to her, but not about another person's success.

The lesson _____ I learned that day was simple: It's possible to be *too* competitive. Sure, competitiveness can help you win a game, but it's not helpful in every situation. Instead, just forget about the envy and be happy for the friends _____ you care about. Don't you want good things to happen to them, too?

Privacy: ● Public   ○ Diary   ○ Friends

Conversation

Track 2-9

A. Listen to the conversation with your book closed. What does the man decide to do?

Dean: Hi, Kirsten. Can I talk to you about something?
Kirsten: Sure. What is it?
Dean: Some of my friends want me to try out for the wrestling team, but I just don't have a competitive personality.
Kirsten: Well, some people are more competitive than others.
Dean: Right, and sometimes I am competitive. I think about my classmates who get good grades and it motivates me to work harder.
Kirsten: There you go.
Dean: On the other hand, very competitive people always want to be the best, but sometimes other people are the best.
Kirsten: And you want to be happy for those other people.
Dean: Exactly! Maybe I could talk to a few guys on the wrestling team and find out if it's the right sport for me.

Real Language

You can say *there you go* when you agree with someone or you think someone has a good idea.

B. Practice the conversation with a partner. Switch roles and practice it again.

 Goal 3   **Talk about positive and negative aspects of competition**

Talk with a partner about times when being competitive is good motivation or simply fun. Then talk about times when being competitive brings out the worst in people.

Reading

A. Read this summary of the article. Use a dictionary to find out the meanings of the words in **blue**.

> You will read about two **anthropologists** from England who wanted to know whether the color of athletes' clothing affected the **outcomes** of sporting events. They did their research during the 2004 Olympic Games in Athens, and they found that wearing the color red was an advantage when the **opponents** had similar abilities—the athletes in red won more often. However, when one athlete was clearly **superior** to the other athlete, the red clothing wasn't important.
>
> The scientists explained these results by looking at the way animals respond to the color red. Some **primates** and birds have red on parts of their bodies, which helps them to attract a **mate**. Another scientist says that **dominant** male animals sometimes have more red on their bodies. The article ends by suggesting that sports **regulations** may need to be changed so that athletes with red uniforms won't have an unfair advantage.

 B. As you read the article, take notes on the scientific research.

the names and university of the scientists who did the research in Athens	
what those scientists wanted to find out	
the method they used (How did they do their research?)	
the results of their research	

 Athens, Greece

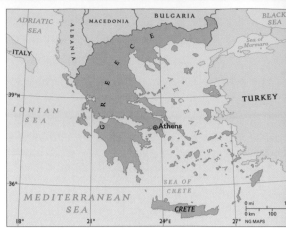

In Sports, Red Is the Winning Color

When **opponents** of a game are equally matched, the team dressed in red is more likely to win, according to a new study.

British **anthropologists** Russell Hill and Robert Barton of the University of Durham reached that conclusion by studying the **outcomes** of boxing, tae kwon do, Greco-Roman wresting, and freestyle wrestling matches at the 2004 Summer Olympics in Athens, Greece.

In each event, Olympic staff randomly assigned red or blue clothing or body protection to competitors. When competitors were equally matched with their opponent in fitness and skill, the athletes wearing red were more likely to win.

"Where there was a large point difference—presumably because one athlete was far **superior** to the other—color had no effect on the outcome," Barton said. "Where there was a small point difference, the effect of color was sufficient to tip the balance."

Joanna Setchell, a primate researcher at the University of Cambridge in England, has found similar results in nature. Her work with the large African monkeys known as mandrills shows that red coloration gives males an advantage when it comes to mating. The finding that red also has an advantage in human sporting events does not surprise her, and she adds that "the idea of the study is very clever."

Hill and Barton got the idea for their study from a mutual interest in **primates**—"red seems to be the color, across species, that signals male dominance," Barton said. For example, studies by Setchell, the Cambridge primate researcher, show that **dominant** male mandrills have increased red coloration in their faces and rumps. In another study, scientists put red plastic rings on the legs of male zebra finches, which increased the birds' success in finding a **mate**.

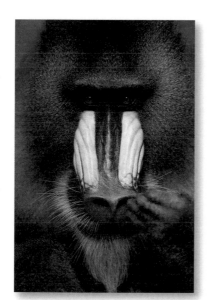

Barton said he and Hill speculated that "there might be a similar effect in humans." Hill and Barton found their answer by viewing Olympic competitors in the ring, on the mat, and in the field. "Across a range of sports, we find that wearing red is consistently associated with a higher probability of winning," the researchers write.

Barton adds that this discovery of red's advantage might lead to new **regulations** on sports uniforms. In the Olympic matches he studied, for example, it is possible that some medal winners may have had an unintended advantage—their clothing!

Engage!

Can studying animals give scientists information about human beings?

C. Read the statements. Circle **T** for *true*, **F** for *false*, or **NI** for *no information* (if the information is not in the reading).

1. Hill and Barton are both interested in primates.   T   F   NI
2. Female mandrills use red coloration to attract a mate.   T   F   NI
3. Red was not an advantage for zebra finches.   T   F   NI
4. The red plastic rings were left on the finches permanently.   T   F   NI
5. Hill and Barton believe athletes in red are more likely to win.   T   F   NI
6. Hill and Barton think some Olympic athletes cheated.   T   F   NI

Writing

A competitive advantage is something that makes you more likely to win or succeed. Besides wearing the color red, what are other things that can give an athlete a competitive advantage? Make a bullet-point list of advice for a coach to give to athletes. Use phrases such as:

- It's a good idea to . . .
- It's absolutely necessary to . . .
- You should always . . .
- Be sure to . . .
- Don't forget to . . .

✓ **Goal 4**   **Discuss competitive advantages**

Read your bullet-point list to a partner and explain how your advice would give an athlete a competitive advantage. Ask your partner to comment on your ideas.

Before You Watch

A. Read about the origins of rodeo competitions. Notice the words in **blue**.

> In the huge, open lands of the American west, herding **cattle** is one way to make a living. The image of the **cowboy** on his horse is a familiar one, but in reality, women also participate in **ranch** work. This reality can be seen in the **rodeo**, where cowboys and cowgirls compete in roping young **steer**, and riding adult **bulls**. Throwing a **rope** around a steer is something ranchers must do in order to give the young animals medicine or to mark the steers as their property. On the other hand, riding on the back of a large and angry bull is purely for sport—a **brutal** and dangerous sport. But that danger doesn't stop the men and women who love the rodeo.

B. Complete the sentences with one of the words in **blue**.

1. A large farm where animals are raised is a _____.
2. _____ are animals that are raised for beef.
3. A man who works on a ranch is sometimes called a _____.
4. Cattle ranchers call one of their young animals a _____.
5. _____ describes something that is cruel and violent.
6. Cattle ranchers call one of their adult male animals a _____.
7. A long, thick cord for tying things together is called a _____.
8. The _____ is a competition that involves ranching skills.

While You Watch

A. Watch the video and check each expression when you hear it.

___ **a man's sport** = a sport that was traditionally played by men
___ **to go head-to-head with someone** = to compete directly with someone
___ **to be in the saddle** = to ride on horseback; to use horses to do one's work
___ **times are changing** = traditional ways are being replaced with new ways
___ **it seems like an eternity** = it seems to take a very long time

 B. Watch the video again and complete each sentence with the word you hear.

1. Meet Debbie Garrison and Pam Midek. They're modern _____ carrying on the ways of the Wild West.
2. As you look at the history of the pioneers of the American West, I think the women were the hardest workers on the _____.
3. Pam and Debbie were riding before they could walk. Their _____ took off when they were crowned Miss Rodeo America.
4. With just seconds to tie horns and legs, team roping is about speed, precision, and _____.
5. Bull riding is the most popular event. It was considered too _____ for women in the past, but times are changing.

After You Watch

 Discuss this quotation from DeDee Crawford, the 2001 world champion female bull rider, with a partner. In your opinion, what do the words tell us about Ms. Crawford?

Communication

Rodeo competitions test the skills of ranchers. Choose one of the jobs below or another job that you know about. Then imagine a new sport that tests the skills people need to do that job. Think of two or three different "events" people can compete in. What must they do to win the events?

school teacher	food server in a restaurant
homemaker	health care worker
taxi driver	police officer

> A lot of times I like to show up, and the guys are like, "There ain't no way she's gonna ride." I like to go out there and do my best and show them I can ride because they think I can't. You've got to keep your head up and say, "I'm just as good as you all are."

DANGER

1. How can people avoid these and other problems with animals?
   a. stings
   b. bites
   c. attacks
   d. scratches

2. What are the most dangerous animals in your country? Why are they dangerous?

UNIT GOALS

Discuss ways to stay safe
Talk about dangerous work
Discuss personal emergencies
Discuss taking risks

UNIT 9

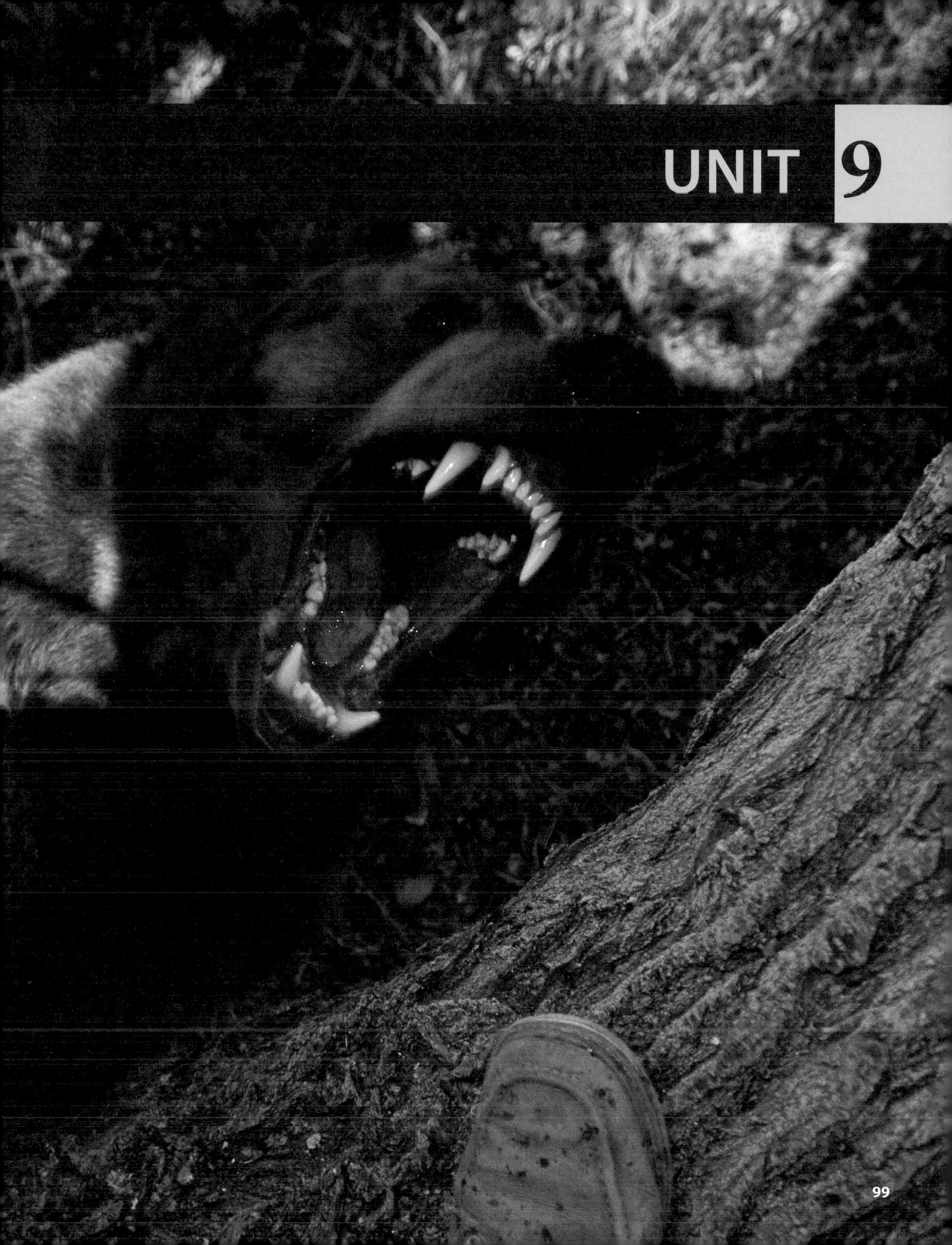

Vocabulary

▲ mosquito

▲ shark

▲ elephant

▲ smoking

▲ alligator

▲ going to bed

A. Look at the pictures and rate them:
   1 = very dangerous,
   2 = somewhat dangerous,
   3 = not dangerous.

B. Read the information below. Which answers would you change in exercise **A**?

> What's *really* dangerous?
> - Scientists **estimate** that mosquitoes kill 3 million people in the world every year.
> - Over 125 deaths a year are caused by elephants (mostly in Africa and Asia).
> - Spiders kill 6 people in the United States every year with their **poison**. The **risk** is higher for children.
> - In the last 60 years, alligators have killed 18 people in Florida.
> - Around the world 1,909 people have been attacked and killed by sharks since 1530—about 5 per year. Many people **survive** shark attacks.
> - Tobacco plays a role in 18.1 percent of all deaths in the United States. It contains over 30 **substances** that are **toxic.**
> - Every year, 36,000 people are **injured** in accidents with their beds. These accidents can be **prevented** easily.

C. Write the words in **blue** next to their meanings.

1. possibility that something bad will happen _____
2. something that kills people if they eat or drink it _____
3. hurt a person's body _____
4. to guess about the number or amount of something _____
5. containing poison _____
6. solids, liquids, or gases _____
7. make sure that something doesn't happen _____
8. live through a dangerous situation _____

Grammar: Tag Questions

Positive sentence, negative tag	Negative sentence, positive tag
Wolves attack people, **don't they**?	Cats don't attack people, **do they**?
You are a student, **aren't you**?	You couldn't swim, **could you**?
It's dangerous, **isn't it**?	He wasn't happy, **was he**?
We won, **didn't we**?	They didn't pass the test, **did they**?
They will be there, **won't they**?	He can't do that, **can he**?
Exception: The tag question for *I am* is *aren't I*?	

* Form tag questions with the auxiliary verb from the main sentence. The subject in the tag question is always a pronoun.
* We usually use a negative tag question after a positive sentence and a positive tag question after a negative sentence.
* We use question tags to check information in the main sentence:
   Those spiders are poisonous, **aren't they**?
* We also use tag questions to ask for agreement:
   He likes snakes, **doesn't he**? (The speaker expects the answer *Yes.*)
   You weren't scared, **were you**? (The speaker expects the answer *No.*)

A. Add tag questions to these sentences.

1. You don't have a car, _____ ?
2. Juan Carlos was late for class yesterday, _____ ?
3. Some kinds of fish are poisonous, _____ ?
4. Susan likes dancing, _____ ?
5. There aren't any dangerous animals in cities, _____ ?
6. Michael can't speak Chinese, _____ ?
7. You'll be here tomorrow, _____ ?
8. Mrs. DaSilva has four children, _____ ?

 B. Talk about these pictures. Use tag questions.

The tiger looks hungry, doesn't he?

Yes, he does! And he . . .

Conversation

 A. Listen to the conversation. Why is the woman worried?

Track 2-10

Ruthie: You know, I really don't like driving. It scares me to death.

Dan: Really? Why is that?

Ruthie: Well, it's dangerous, isn't it? Just think of all the people who are killed in their cars every year!

Dan: That's nothing to worry about. There's a lot you can do to stay safe.

Ruthie: Like what?

Dan: For one thing, you should stop talking on your cell phone when you drive. That causes a lot of accidents.

Ruthie: I suppose you're right.

Dan: And you should keep enough distance from other cars.

Ruthie: That's not a bad idea.

Engage!

What scares you to death?

 B. What can you do to stay safe in these situations? Think of several ideas with a partner. Then make new conversations.

thunderstorms   flying on an airplane   fixing the roof

✓ **Goal 1   Discuss ways to stay safe**

Talk to your partner about how to stay safe in another situation.

Rajasthan, India

Listening

Track 2-11

A. Listen to a radio program about an unusual job. Then read the statements and choose the correct answer.

1. The job of a food taster is to make sure that food is ____.
   a. delicious   b. healthy   c. not poisoned

2. Today, there are ____ food tasters.
   a. no more   b. only a few   c. many

Track 2-11

B. Listen again. Then fill in each space with one word to make a summary of the radio program.

In the past, kings and queens used food tasters to protect themselves against _____. Their job was to taste all the food in the king's meal and make sure it was _____ to eat. Mathura Prasad was a food taster for the lord of Castle Mandawa in _____. When the food was ready, some of it was fed to a _____. Then Mathura Prasad _____ it before it went to the lord's table. Food tasters have a long _____. For example, Christopher Columbus used _____ to test food on his trips. Today, most countries don't use food tasters, but in _____ soldiers sometimes taste the president's food. And in _____, the king's food is checked by mice.

▲ Mathura Prasad, food taster to the *thakur*, or lord, of Castle Mandawa

C. Discuss the questions with a partner.

1. What are the good points and bad points of Mathura Prasad's job?
2. Why do you think he did this job?

Pronunciation: Intonation of tag questions

Track 2-12

A. The intonation of tag questions shows how sure we are of the answer. If we are very sure of the answer and want agreement, we use falling intonation. If we are not sure of the answer and want to check the information, we use rising intonation. Listen and repeat the sentences, noticing the intonation.

1. Mathura had a dangerous job, didn't he? (sure)
2. There aren't many food tasters now, are there? (not sure)

B. Listen to the statements and circle *sure* or *not sure*. Then practice reading them to a partner.

1.	That plant isn't poisonous, is it?	sure	not sure
2.	He knows all about it, doesn't he?	sure	not sure
3.	That bridge doesn't look safe, does it?	sure	not sure
4.	You were here yesterday, weren't you?	sure	not sure
5.	His name is David, isn't it?	sure	not sure
6.	This exercise was easy, wasn't it?	sure	not sure

Communication

A. Look at the photos of dangerous jobs and fill in as many ideas as you can.

	Description	Bad things about the job	Good things about the job
	firefighter: puts out fires in houses and other buildings	-could be burned -have to work really fast	-save people's lives
	race car driver:		
	tiger trainer:		

B. Role-play a newspaper reporter interviewing the people in exercise **A**. Use tag questions to check information and add your own ideas.

> You run into burning buildings, don't you?

> That's right. It's incredibly hot in there!

✓ **Goal 2** | **Talk about dangerous work**

Discuss the questions with a partner.

1. Would you like to do any of the jobs in exercise A? Why, or why not?
2. What other jobs are dangerous? Why?
3. Why are people attracted to dangerous jobs?

Language Expansion: Expressions for emergencies

A. What should you say? Write the correct sentence for each picture.

| Where's the nearest pharmacy? | Where's the emergency room? | Where's the nearest hospital? |
| Call the police! | Call the fire department! | Call an ambulance! | Call a doctor! |

1. _____ 2. _____ 3. _____

4. _____ 5. _____ 6. _____ 7. _____

B. Think of one more situation for each of the sentences in exercise **A**.

> If your child swallows something toxic, you should ask, "Where's the nearest hospital?"

Grammar: Adverbial clauses of time

Main clause	Adverbial clause
They ran out of the house	**when** they saw the fire.
The ambulance will come	**as soon as** it can get here.
She buys DVDs	**whenever** she has extra money.
I finished my project	**before** I went home.
Jack called his mother	**after** he ate dinner.

*Adverbial clauses give more information about the main verb of the sentence. An adverbial clause of time answers the question *When?*
* The adverbial clause can come before or after the main clause. If the adverbial clause comes before the main clause, it is followed by a comma.
*I finished my project **before I went home**./**Before I went home**, I finished my project.*

A. Underline the adverbial clause. Then rewrite the sentence with the adverbial clause first.

1. I take a shower and eat breakfast <u>before I go to class</u>. *Before* _____

   _____

2. He called the fire department as soon as he saw the flames. _____

   _____

3. We feel nervous whenever we have a test. _____

   _____

4. I like to watch the news on TV while I eat breakfast. _____

   _____

5. I screamed when I saw the snake. _____

   _____

 B. What should you do in these situations? Talk about what to do, forming adverbial clauses with *when*, *as soon as*, *whenever*, *before*, and *after*.

> When you see a car accident, you should call the police.
>
> And after you call the police . . .

| see a car accident | meet a bear in the woods | smell smoke in a building | run into a poisonous snake |

Conversation

Track 2-14

A. Listen to the phone conversation with your book closed. What was the problem at Jen's house?

Jen: Hello?

Lily: Hi Jen, it's Lily, your neighbor . . . are you OK? I saw the fire truck in front of your house!

Jen: Don't worry, we're fine. We had a fire in our kitchen, but everything's OK now.

Lily: Oh, no! What happened?

Jen: I was cooking dinner, and I went to check on the baby. When I went back, the kitchen was full of black smoke!

Lily: How awful!

Jen: As soon as I saw the smoke, I called the fire department. After I called them, I took the baby out of the house.

Lily: Did it take them long to get there?

Jen: Only a few minutes. They put out the fire before it got very far. But my whole house smells like smoke now.

Lily: I'm so glad you're OK!

 B. Practice the conversation with a partner.

Goal 3 **Discuss personal emergencies**

Tell a partner about an emergency or serious problem that you had.

Real Language

We say *Oh no!* or *How awful!* when someone tells us about something very bad that happened.

Reading

 A. Discuss the questions with a partner.

1. What are some dangerous activities that people do for fun?
2. Would you like to try any of these activities? Why, or why not?

 B. Read the statements. Circle **T** for *true*, **F** for *false*, and **NI** for *no information* (if the answer is not in the reading).

1. Fugu are a kind of poisonous fish.   T F NI
2. People in Japan eat fugu because it's very cheap.   T F NI
3. Restaurants in Japan aren't allowed to sell some parts of a fugu.   T F NI
4. Fugu live only in the sea around Japan.   T F NI
5. Scientists know exactly where the toxins in fugu come from.   T F NI
6. A scientist has produced fugu that aren't dangerous.   T F NI
7. Fugu is safe to eat after it is cooked.   T F NI

C. Match the sentence parts to show the reasons.

1. Fugu chefs must pass a difficult test ___.
2. People like to eat fugu liver ___.
3. Selling fugu liver is not allowed in Japan ___.
4. Fugu must be prepared carefully ___.
5. Noguchi did experiments with fugu ___.

  a. to produce fugu with no toxins
  b. because only some parts are safe to eat
  c. because it makes the mouth tingle
  d. because their mistakes can kill people
  e. because it is too dangerous

 Tokyo, Japan

A Delicacy to Die For

samurai sword

puffer fish (fugu)

chef

sashimi

Fugu, or **puffer** fish, is a famous and exotic food in Japan. It can also be deadly. People who eat the liver, skin, or some other body parts of the fish swallow a poison called tetrodoxin, which stops human nerve cells from working. They risk dying—just like a famous Japanese actor named Mitsuguro Bando. In 1975, he spent an evening with friends eating fugu liver, because he enjoyed the tingling feeling it created in his mouth. But that tingling was caused by the poison. Soon, Bando couldn't move his arms or legs. Then he had trouble breathing. Eight hours later, he was dead.

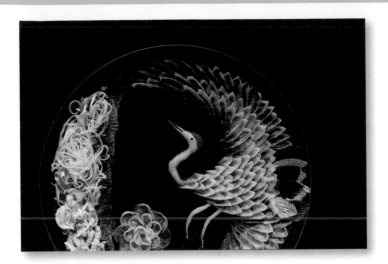

You can still eat fugu in Japan in restaurants where **chefs** prepare beautiful plates of thinly sliced raw fugu for $500. Fortunately, nowadays, fugu chefs must have training and a special license. They have to pass an exam: in 20 minutes, they must divide a fish into edible and toxic parts, label the parts with plastic tags (black for edible, red for toxic), make it into **sashimi**, and prepare a beautiful arrangement on a plate. Last year, 900 candidates took the exam, but only 63 percent of them passed. They are not allowed to serve the liver or other toxic parts.

Scientists are not sure about the origin of the fugu's poison. Tamao Noguchi, a researcher at Nagasaki University, believes that the secret is in the fugu's diet. Puffer fish, he explains, take in toxins when they eat smaller animals like worms or shellfish that contain toxic bacteria. In experiments, Noguchi raised several fugu in his laboratory and fed them a special diet. Their bodies did not contain the toxin.

Noguchi hopes that his research will make fugu liver available in restaurants in the future. "It's a great delicacy," he says. "Once you eat it, you cannot stop." Japan banned the sale of fugu liver in 1983, because hundreds of people had died from eating just a little too much of it or eating it by mistake. If Noguchi can produce nontoxic fugu, the laws could be changed.

But would nontoxic fugu really be the same? Some people think the taste would be just as delicious. But Noguchi says it would actually be a sad day for the fish. "After all," he says, "a fugu without its poison is like a **samurai** without his **sword**."

Communication

👥 Discuss the questions with two or more students.

1. Why do you think people like to eat fugu? List all the reasons you can think of.
2. Why do some people enjoy doing risky things?
3. Tell the group about a time when you took a risk. How did you feel? Are you glad that you did it?

Writing

Write about the experience you described to your group. Include details about what you did and your reasons for doing it.

✓ **Goal 4** **Discuss taking risks**

Do you enjoy taking risks? Explain your answer to a partner.

Before You Watch

👥 Look at the pictures. Are any of these appliances dangerous? How could they be dangerous?

▲ iron

▲ toaster

▲ blender

▲ hair dryer

While You Watch

A. Watch the video and circle the answers.

1. The employees at Underwriters Laboratories (UL) try to (make/destroy) new products.
2. The purpose of UL is to see if appliances will be (safe/popular).
3. UL is a/an (new/old) company.
4. Some people think the work of UL is (funny/dangerous).

B. Watch the video again. Circle **T** for *true* and **F** for *false*.

1. Underwriters Laboratory was started in 1994.	T	F
2. Some of the tests at UL are the same as in the past.	T	F
3. The *drop test* is a test for appliances.	T	F
4. Engineers at UL only test the correct way to use an appliance.	T	F
5. At the end of the day, UL employees can keep the appliances.	T	F
6. Employees sometimes call UL *the Fun House*.	T	F

 C. Watch the video again. Fill in the missing words.

1. Many of the people who work here are highly trained _____ .
2. Each year, thousands of home appliances are _____ .
3. This is to make them safe for people who don't use them _____ .
4. These funny tests have a very serious purpose: to _____ people from accidents that could happen.
5. The engineers must predict all the ways people could use an appliance
   _____ .
6. At the end of the workday, UL employees collect the _____ from the day's experiments.

After You Watch

 Discuss these questions with a partner.

1. Why do people have accidents at home?
2. If a person uses a product wrong and gets hurt, who is responsible? The person or the maker of the product? Explain your reasons.

Communication

 Imagine you are a group of safety engineers, like the ones in the video. Choose a common appliance. Make a list of ways that people might use this appliance wrong, and plan the tests that you will do. Share your ideas with the class. (DON'T do any real tests!)

MYSTERIES

1. What do you think of when you hear the word *mysteries*?

2. What kinds of mysteries do these pictures represent?

UNIT GOALS

Speculate about mysteries
Discuss types of mysteries you like and dislike
Talk about plans you used to have
Explain a mysterious image

UNIT 10

Vocabulary

A. Read about mysteries. Notice the words in **blue**.

For every mystery, there is someone trying to **figure out** what happened. Scientists, detectives, and ordinary people **search** for **evidence** that will help to reveal the truth. They **investigate prehistoric** sites trying to understand how and why ancient people **constructed** pyramids or created strange artwork. They study the **remains** of long-extinct animals and they **speculate** about how the animals might have looked when they were alive. Anything that is unexplained is fascinating to people who love a mystery.

B. Write the words in **blue** next to their correct meanings.

1. clues that make you believe something is true _____
2. to make guesses about something _____
3. to look carefully for something or someone _____
4. the parts of something that are left after most of it is gone _____
5. to solve or understand something _____
6. built, made, or created something _____
7. to try to find out what happened or what is true _____
8. describes people or things that existed before information was written down _____

Word Focus

Two verb + preposition combinations you should know are **search for**, and **speculate about**.

Grammar: Modals for speculating about the past

Modals for speculating about the past
subject + modal + *have* + past participle
* When we speculate or make guesses about the past, we use *may*, *might*, or *could*. 　The explorers **may have died** in a shipwreck. 　The object **might have been** a UFO. 　Marco **could have helped** the bank robber. *When we are almost certain about our speculation or guess, we use *must*. 　They **must have left** the beach when it started raining.

Fill in each blank with the correct form of the verb in parentheses and an appropriate modal from the chart.

1. We don't know who robbed the bank, but we think the robber _____ (enter) the bank through a small window.
2. We don't know what happened to Amelia Earhart, but we think her plane _____ (crash) on an island in the Pacific.
3. I don't know where my keys are, but I _____ (have) them with me when I left the apartment because the door is locked.
4. We don't think it was really a UFO. It _____ (be) an unusual cloud or a large balloon.
5. I don't know what time he got home, but he _____ (sleep) in his bed because the sheets and pillow are rumpled.
6. No one knows what happened to the treasure ship, but some people think it _____ (sink) in the Mediterranean Sea.

> The workers might have put the stones on boats on the Nile River.

Communication

 A. Talk about these famous places. Use modals for speculating about the past.

1. The pyramids at Giza, Egypt, are the subject of much speculation. The largest of the three pyramids was completed some 4,500 years ago and was made from over 2 million huge stone blocks. How do you think workers constructed these pyramids?

2. The Nazca lines in Peru are a group of enormous pictures made by removing reddish surface stones to expose the light-colored ground below. Because of their large size, it's impossible to see any one of the pictures from the ground, and there are no nearby mountains. What do you think was the purpose of these pictures?

3. On Easter Island in the Pacific Ocean, hundreds of stone statues called *moai* stand near the shore and stare out to sea. No one is sure about the meaning of the statues. What do you think the meaning might have been?

B. Talk to a partner about mysterious places in your country. Why are the places mysterious?

✓ Goal 1 — Speculate about mysteries

Talk to a partner. Choose one of the mysteries pictured in the unit opener or in this lesson and take turns speculating about it.

▲ Nessie

▲ Unktehila

▲ Chinese dragons

Listening

 A. Discuss the questions with a partner.

1. Do you know any stories about sea monsters?
2. Do you think sea monsters might really exist?
3. Do you know what fossils are?

Track 2-15

B. Listen to an expert talking about sea monsters. Write the name of a place under each monster.

Track 2-15

C. Listen again and choose the correct answer to each question.

1. According to the expert, at one time, sea monsters _____.
   a. didn't exist   b. might have existed   c. did exist
2. When scientists found fossils near Loch Ness, people speculated that Nessie might be _____.
   a. a skeleton   b. a dinosaur   c. a rock
3. According to legends, the Unktehila were destroyed by _____.
   a. snakes   b. Native Americans   c. Thunder Beings
4. Millions of years ago, _____ lived in North America.
   a. alligators   b. mosasaurs   c. crocodiles
5. Some Chinese dragons represented good luck because they could _____.
   a. bring rain   b. find fossils   c. sail in boats

Track 2-15

D. Listen again. Then discuss the questions with a partner.

1. Which sea monster story was the most interesting to you?
2. If you could talk to the expert, what questions would you ask?

Engage!

Why do people enjoy mysteries?

Pronunciation: Intonation: Finished and unfinished ideas

Track 2-16

A. In a conversation, it's important to know when someone has finished speaking. One way speakers show that they are finished is falling intonation. When they are not finished, they may use steady or rising intonation. Listen to these finished and unfinished ideas.

Finished	Unfinished
He thought he saw something in the water.	At first he thought it was a fish, . . .
These stories can't possibly be true.	But some people believe them, . . .

Track 2-17

B. When you hear an unfinished idea, the speaker may plan to continue. Listen to the examples.

C. Practice the sentences with a partner. End the sentence with steady or rising intonation when you see three dots (. . .). End with falling intonation when you see a period (.).

1. Loch Ness is 37 kilometers long and very deep.
2. The pilot said he saw a large object flying beside the airplane.
3. The ship's captain tried to send a radio message, . . .
4. People see different things when they look at the painting.
5. Some people may have dreams about the future, . . .

D. For each unfinished idea in exercise **C**, speculate about what the speaker will say next.

Conversation

Track 2-18

A. Listen to the conversation with your book closed. Why does the man think the woman won't like the book?

Joan: Hi, Tommy. What are you reading?
Tommy: It's a mystery novel—*The Clock Strikes at Midnight*.
Joan: Is it any good?
Tommy: It's all right, . . .
Joan: Then maybe I'll read it when you're done.
Tommy: Maybe not. I was going to say it's good, but I don't think you'd like it.
Joan: Why not? I like mystery novels.
Tommy: I know, but in this one, a young child is missing. I know you don't like to read about kidnappings, or murder, or . . .
Joan: You're right. It doesn't sound like my kind of book.

> **Real Language**
>
> We can say *It's (not) my kind of X* to talk about things we like or dislike.

B. Practice the conversation with a partner. Then switch roles and practice it again.

Goal 2 **Discuss types of mysteries you like and dislike**

Some people like a good ghost story. Others enjoy murder mysteries. Tell a partner about the kinds of mysteries you enjoy hearing about or reading about. Then talk about mysterious things that you'd rather not hear or read about.

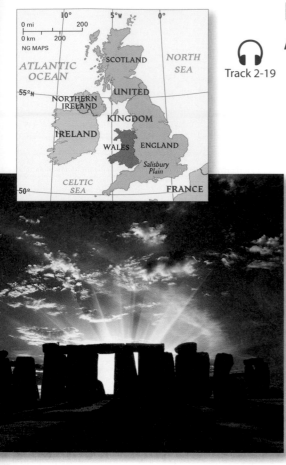

Language Expansion: Reacting to surprises

Track 2-19

A. Listen to a tour guide talk about Stonehenge, a prehistoric grouping of huge stones in southern England. Fill in the blanks as you listen.

Tour guide: You can see that Stonehenge is very old. In fact, people started constructing Stonehenge nearly _____ years ago.

Tourist: Wow!

Tour guide: That's right. And while no one really knows why Stonehenge was constructed, there are some things we do know. The largest stones you see are these *trilithons*—two huge upright stones with a third stone laid on top. On average, these stones are _____ meters high.

Tourist: That's amazing!

Tour guide: I agree. What's even more amazing is that prehistoric people transported these stones _____ kilometers. And that was without any modern machinery.

Tourist: Really!

Tour guide: And would you believe that these smaller bluestones came from a site in Wales, around _____ kilometers away!

Tourist: You're kidding!

Tour guide: I'm not! And the builders of Stonehenge must have known a lot about transportation because each of these "smaller" stones weighs around _____ kilos!

Tourist: Remarkable!

Track 2-19

B. Listen again and notice the way the tourists express their surprise.

C. Take turns. Tell your classmates about mysterious things you know about. Your classmates will use some of the expressions from activity **A** to show their surprise.

Grammar: The future in the past

The future in the past
subject + *was/were* + *going to* + verb

*We use this structure to talk about future plans that were made at a past time.
    *His friends **were going to** walk to school that day.*
 *This structure often means that the plans did not actually happen.
    *Samir **was going to** take the bus, but he changed his mind.*

A. Fill in the blanks to complete the future-in-the-past structure.

In 1501, the Portuguese explorer Gaspar Corte-Real left Portugal with three ships. He _____ search for a route to India. He sailed northwest, and although he didn't reach India, he did find a land he called Terra Verde, or Greenland. Then all three ships sailed south. They _____ return to Portugal. Unfortunately, only two ships arrived in Lisbon. Corte-Real's ship was never seen again.

Then in 1502, Gaspar's brother Miguel Corte-Real set out on an expedition with two ships. He _____ look for his brother. Unfortunately, no one knows whether he found Gaspar. After sailing for some time, Miguel had the two ships go separate ways, thinking they _____ cover more area and have a better chance of locating Gaspar. But Miguel's ship never returned to Portugal.

That left one surviving brother, Vasco Annes, who asked the king for permission to launch a third expedition. He _____ do what Miguel had failed to do—find his brother. Perhaps wisely, King Manuel refused to give Vasco Annes permission for the journey.

Conversation

Track 2-20

A. Listen to the conversation with your book closed. What kind of actress did the woman want to be when she was a child?

Angela: I can't believe that science classes are so hard for me! When I was a child, I wanted to be an archaeologist.

Yada: Don't be so hard on yourself. You can still be an archaeologist if you want to.

Angela: Thanks. I probably am being too hard on myself.

Yada: I was going to be a famous actress.

Angela: An actress! Were you going to be in the movies or on TV?

Yada: Oh, on the stage! I went to see a play one time, and I just knew I was going to work in the theater when I grew up.

Angela: Well, maybe you still can.

Yada: I don't think so. Now I want to be a politician.

Angela: You're kidding! A politician?

Yada: Sure. Politicians and actresses both need to be great speakers.

Angela: You're right about that. Maybe I should come up with a new career plan, too.

B. Practice the conversation with a partner. Then switch roles and practice it again.

✓ **Goal 3** **Talk about plans you used to have**

Tell a partner about plans you had for the future when you were a child. What were you going to be when you grew up? Where were you going to live? What was your life going to be like?

▲ Luc-Henri Fage

Reading

A. Discuss the questions with a partner.

1. When you imagine scientists at work, where do you see them?
2. Do you think it's important to learn about prehistoric people?

B. Try to figure out the meaning of each word in bold without using a dictionary.

1. trek _____
2. facing _____
3. handprints _____
4. shamanistic _____
5. fragile _____

C. What do you think the scientists wondered when they first saw the Kalimantan cave paintings? Write three questions they might have asked themselves.

1. _____
2. _____
3. _____

D. Compare your questions with a partner's questions. Then speculate about the possible answers.

☐ Indonesian Borneo

Hands Across Time

They're known as *cavers*—people whose idea of a good time is exploring dark and sometimes dangerous caves. And that was exactly what first drew Luc-Henri Fage to the Island of Borneo in 1988. His goal at the time was an adventurous **trek** across the island along with other cavers.

On that first trip to Borneo, Luc-Henri saw ancient charcoal drawings on the ceiling of a large rock overhang. When he returned to France, he couldn't find any information about rock art in the region, so he returned to Borneo. Over the years he kept returning and was joined by a French archaeologist and an Indonesian anthropologist. They found numerous caves with not only drawings, but also mysterious and obviously very old paintings. Then in 1999, they saw the hands for the first time.

Exploring the region of Kalimantan, the Indonesian part of Borneo, is not an easy task. There are no roads to the Marang Mountains, so Fage and the others made their way up the Bungulun River in canoes, camping along the way, at times **facing** storms and fire ants that tried to join the campers to get out of the rain. The Marang Mountains rise out of the hot, humid jungle below, and their steep sides hold the caves that first brought Fage here. The rock art is found in the highest of these caves, often painted on a very high ceiling. As Fage points out, "If something goes wrong, you die."

One large cave contains drawings of humans and animals, and around 350 images of **handprints**, some of them covered in patterns that look something like tattoos or body painting.

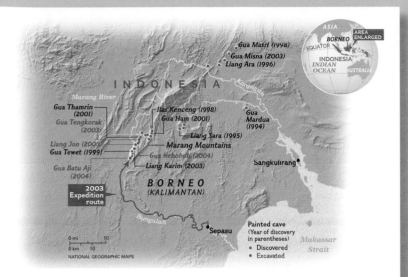

Fage has counted 57 types of symbols depicted on the hands and is working hard to decode their meaning. Since the caves don't contain evidence of people living in them, it's likely that they were used for ceremonial or spiritual purposes. "We're dealing with **shamanistic** practices here . . . but I'm not sure what kind," says archaeologist Jean-Michel Chazine. The team thinks that the people who created these works of art more than 10,000 years ago may have been related to the aboriginal people of Australia.

Like cave paintings everywhere, the ones in Borneo are very **fragile**, and many of them may have already disappeared due to weather and time. The scientific community has learned about them only recently and is working to provide information that could lead to the protection of the rock art. Currently, Fage and Chazine display photos of the rock art and give information in French and English on their Web site, *www.kalimanthrope.com*. It's a place in cyberspace where anyone in the world can learn more about the mysterious caves of Kalimantan.

Communication

Amazing photographs are easy to find on the Internet, but since images can be changed with computer software programs, you can't always believe what you see. Talk to a partner about these two pictures. Try to agree on which image is real and which is an example of *fauxtography*—a photograph that's designed to deceive the viewer.

◄ sandstorm in Iraq

◄ iceberg in the Atlantic Ocean

Writing

Write a paragraph about each picture. Briefly describe the image, then explain how the photograph was taken or changed to get the effect you see.

✓ Goal 4 | **Explain a mysterious image**

Take turns. Read your paragraphs to a partner. Try to agree on the best explanation for each image.

England, U.K.

Before You Watch

A. Discuss these questions with a partner.

1. Is there any evidence that aliens from outer space visit earth?
2. If aliens could visit earth, how would they get here?
3. If aliens could visit earth, what would they do here?

B. What do you think? Check the sentences you agree with.

1. ___ There may be forms of intelligent life in the universe besides humans.
2. ___ Crop circles are probably made by aliens from outer space.
3. ___ It's strange that crop circles only occur in England.
4. ___ Crop circles are probably made by human beings.
5. ___ It's impossible for humans to make these large geometric designs.

While You Watch

A. Watch the video and complete each statement to show the person's opinion.

Reg Presley, Crop Circle Researcher:

I think that most crop circles

are probably man-made, but

_____

Matthew, Crop Circle Maker:

Some people believe its not

possible for human beings to

make these crop circles, but

_____

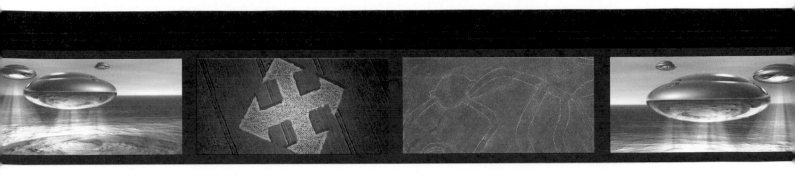

 B. Read the video summary and fill in each blank with a word from the box. Then watch the video again and check your answers.

| other-worldly puzzle boards mortals phenomenon markers |

Video Summary

This video examines crop circles, a strange _____ that occurs in England. These complex designs appear mysteriously in farmers' fields overnight, and people want to know if they're made by _____ such as you and me, or if the circles are _____ messages from aliens. To one researcher, crop circles are a _____—a mystery that he would like to solve. For one crop circle maker, on the other hand, there is no mystery. He thinks that artists and graphic designers make the crop circles using flat _____ to flatten the grain and _____ to help them create the designs.

Communication

 Discuss these questions with a partner.

1. What surprised you the most about the video?
2. What do you still want to know about crop circles?

After You Watch

Think of some questions you would like to ask the crop circle makers. Then, since we're not sure who makes the circles, finish the letters below with different questions.

| Dear alien crop circle maker,
Your designs are very beautiful, and I hope you won't mind if I ask you a few questions about them. First,

_____
_____
_____ | Dear human crop circle maker,
Your designs are very beautiful, and I hope you won't mind if I ask you a few questions about them. First,

_____
_____
_____ |

LEARNING

1. Which of these kinds of learning experiences have you participated in? What did you study?
   a. study tour
   b. practical experience
   c. demonstration
   d. lecture

2. What is the best way for you to learn?

UNIT GOALS

Talk about educational plans and decisions
Discuss your learning style
Talk about choosing a university major
Propose a new approach to teaching

Vocabulary

A. Read the article. Write the words in **blue** next to their meanings.

> **Study Abroad Programs: SEA Semester**
>
> For students who want to spend a **semester** away from their **campus**, the SEA Semester is a wonderful opportunity. Thirty-five students spend six weeks in Massachusetts, USA, taking **courses** about biology and the sea—and then use what they learned on a six-week trip on a small sailing ship, doing research with professional scientists. Each year, SEA Semester ships travel around the Atlantic and the Pacific. Students from colleges and universities in many countries **enroll** in the program. The **tuition** is not cheap—about $16,000—but **scholarships** are available. You don't have to have a science **major**, and sailing experience is not a **requirement**. You do have to **apply** very early, though—the **deadline** is six months before the program starts.

1. money given to good students to pay for their studies _____
2. main subject that you are studying _____
3. a series of lessons or lectures about a subject _____
4. the last day to do something _____
5. to fill out a form to ask for something _____
6. money you pay to study _____
7. an area of land with college or university buildings _____
8. something that you must have or do to be suitable for something _____
9. to join a school or a class _____
10. half of a school year _____

B. Discuss the questions with a partner.

1. What are the good points and bad points of this program?
2. Would you like to participate in this program? Why, or why not?

> I love the ocean.

> Yes, but six weeks is a long time on a small ship!

Grammar: *Should have, could have, would have*

I didn't apply for a scholarship.	I **should have** applied for a scholarship.
I missed the deadline	I **shouldn't have** missed the deadline.
I didn't talk to my teacher.	I **could have** talked to my teacher.
You didn't ask me for help.	I **would have** helped you.

* Perfect modals can be used to talk about actions that weren't realized in the past.
* **should have** = this was a good idea, but I didn't do it: I **should have** gone to bed earlier.
* **shouldn't have** = this was a bad idea, but I did it: I **shouldn't have** gotten angry at the children.
* **could have** = this was possible, but I didn't do it. I **could have** studied abroad, but I stayed home.
* **would have** = I was willing to do this, but I didn't do it. I **would have** given you some money.

A. Complete the sentences. Use *should (not) have*, *could have*, or *would have* with a verb from the box.

give	shout	practice	go	~~spend~~	say	buy

1. We _shouldn't have spent_ so much money last week. Now we don't have enough to pay the bills.
2. I didn't know you were going to the meeting. I _____ you a ride there.
3. I _____ to three different parties last night, but I was tired, so I just stayed home.
4. Andrew failed his driving test yesterday. He _____ more before he took the test.
5. That was a terrible idea. Kayla _____ at our boss like that.
6. I _____ hello to you in the coffee shop, but I didn't see you in the corner.
7. Mike's girlfriend is upset because he forgot her birthday. He really _____ her a present!

 B. Talk with your partner about these things. Use *should have*, *could have*, or *would have*.

1. a bad decision that you made
2. an experience that you didn't try

> I could have lived in London for a year.
>> Really!? Why didn't you go?

Conversation

 A. Listen to the conversation with your book closed. Where does Josh want to study next year?

Track 2-21

Kelly: Hi, Josh. What's up?

Josh: Not much. I have to study. I need to review 30 Japanese words for my quiz tomorrow, and they all look the same.

Kelly: You really picked a tough major!

Josh: The big problem is that I don't get many chances to speak the language. My college has a summer program in Tokyo. I should have applied for that.

Kelly: Why didn't you?

Josh: Because I missed the deadline! I could have spent two months in Japan. I would have studied 12 hours a day . . .

Kelly: Well, don't worry about it. I'm sure you'll have other chances.

Josh: Yeah, you're right. If I get good grades, there's an exchange program. I could spend next year at a Japanese university. I'm definitely going to apply.

 B. Practice the conversation with a partner.

Goal 1   Talk about educational plans and decisions

Make new conversations about these things:
a. studying art history in Rome   b. (your own idea)

Listening

A. Read the article.

Learning Styles
What is the best way to learn new information? Researchers have found that each person has a learning style they prefer. There are four different kinds of learners.

Auditory learners	Visual learners	Kinesthetic learners	Reading/ writing learners
prefer to get information by listening. They like to learn through lectures, group discussion, and conversations.	like to take in new information by seeing. Photos, charts, drawings, and diagrams help them to understand new ideas.	understand things best through experience and practice. They like to make things and use their bodies.	understand new information best when they read or write words. Using a textbook and reading articles are activities they prefer.

Track 2-22

B. Listen to three speakers talk about their learning experiences. What did each person study?

Speaker 1: _____

Speaker 2: _____

Speaker 3: _____

Track 2-22

C. Listen to the speakers again. What is each person's learning style?

Speaker 1:

auditory visual kinesthetic reading/writing

Speaker 2:

auditory visual kinesthetic reading/writing

Speaker 3:

auditory visual kinesthetic reading/writing

Pronunciation: Past modals

Track 2-23

A. Listen to the sentences with past modals. Notice how *would have/could have/ should have* sound like *woulda/coulda/shoulda*.

1. I should have saved my money.
2. I could have just stayed home.
3. I would have bought something like that a long time ago.

 B. Read these sentences to a partner. Pay attention to the pronunciation of past modals.

1. Our teacher should have told us about the quiz.
2. He must have forgotten about the meeting.
3. I would have helped you wash the dishes.
4. They could have studied in England last year.
5. She might have been absent that day.
6. You should have bought her a present.

Communication

 A. Give a partner this learning style quiz. Read the questions to your partner, and circle his or her answers. Then check your partner's score.

1. If I don't know how to spell a word, I
   a. pronounce it slowly.
   b. try to see the word in my mind.
   c. write it several ways and choose one.
   d. look it up in the dictionary.
2. If I need directions to a place, I like people to
   a. tell me the directions.
   b. draw a map for me.
   c. take me there.
   d. write the directions for me.
3. If I have problems installing a new computer printer, I
   a. call someone to ask questions.
   b. look at a diagram.
   c. experiment until I figure it out.
   d. read the instructions.

4. I prefer classes that have lots of
   a. lectures and discussion.
   b. pictures and diagrams.
   c. field trips and projects.
   d. books and reading.
5. When I study for a test, I like to
   a. have someone ask me questions.
   b. look at charts and pictures.
   c. make note cards and models.
   d. go over the textbook again.

Your score: If you have three or more A answers: you are an auditory learner. If you have three or more B answers: you are a visual learner. If you have three or more C answers: you are a kinesthetic learner. If you have three or more D answers: you are a reading/writing learner.

 B. Discuss the questions with two or three students.

1. What was your preferred learning style from the quiz? Does that description fit you?
2. How can people with different learning styles learn these things?
   Italian cooking   the names of 50 kinds of birds   (your group's idea)

> I should have made a cassette of my vocabulary words!

✓ **Goal 2** **Discuss your learning style**

Think of a time when you had problems learning something. How could you have used knowledge of learning styles to help?

Language Expansion: University majors

A. These university students are talking about their majors. Read what they say, and write the major from the box.

economics	education	agriculture	law	~~business~~
engineering	psychology	chemistry	social work	geology

1. I'm studying why some companies are so successful. **Major:** _business_
2. Our professor talked about why people have legal problems. **Major:** _____
3. I'm learning about how the money system works. **Major:** _____
4. Our class today was about where petroleum and metals are found in the earth.
   Major: _____
5. In class, we talk about why some children learn more slowly. **Major:** _____
6. We study how we can help poor people. **Major:** _____
7. I had a lecture about where farm plants grow well in our country. **Major:** _____
8. In my major, I learn how I can help people with mental problems. **Major:** _____
9. We are studying how new chemicals are made in a laboratory. **Major:** _____
10. I've learned why some roads and bridges last for a long time. **Major:** _____

> My major was history. I took a lot of courses about . . .

 B. Discuss the questions with a partner.

1. What is your major? (*or* What will your major be?/What was your major?)
2. What are some things that people learn when they study that major?

Grammar: Noun clauses

I'm interested in	education. **how** children learn.	I don't know	the deadline. **when** the form is due.
Do you remember	the reason? **why** she called?	I enjoyed	his lecture. **what** he talked about.

* A noun clause can take the place of a noun in a sentence.
* Form noun clauses with a *wh-* word, a subject, and a verb.
* Noun clauses can be used in different parts of the sentence.
Subject: ***What you said*** *was very interesting.*
Object: *I liked **what you said**.*
After a preposition: *I'll think about **what you said**.*

A. Write answers with noun clauses.

1. Where are my keys?
   I don't know <u>where your keys are</u>

2. What did he talk about?
   I don't remember _____ .

3. When is the meeting?
   Nobody told me _____ .

4. Where does Katie live?
   I'm not really sure _____ .

5. Why did John get so angry?
   I can't understand _____ .

6. How do you pronounce that word?
   I have no idea _____ .

 B. Take turns asking a partner these questions. Use noun clauses in your answer.

1. What are some things you're curious about?
2. What was your favorite class in elementary school? What did you learn about?
3. Are you worried about anything? What do you worry about?

Conversation

 A. Listen to the conversation with your book closed. What two majors is Annie thinking about?

Track 2-24

> In history class, the teacher talked about how people lived in the past.

Mike: What's the matter, Annie? You look worried.

Annie: I guess I am. I just got a letter from the university, and it said the deadline for choosing my major is Friday.

Mike: You mean, you still haven't decided?

Annie: It's so hard to make up my mind! Psychology is interesting because you learn why people do things. But if I studied social work, I would actually learn to help families with problems.

Mike: Well, maybe you should think about what you do in class.

Annie: What do you mean?

Mike: You know, you don't like reading very much, and a psychology major has to read tons of books.

Annie: That's a good point. And I really like classes where you work together with other people.

Mike: So it sounds like social work is a better major for you.

Annie: I think you're right.

Real Language

We use *You mean* . . . to check if we understood what someone just said.

Word Focus

make up my mind = decide

 B. Practice the conversation with a partner. Then make new conversations about these majors.

a. history and education   b. English and business

Goal 3 **Talk about choosing a university major**

Make a new conversation about two majors that interest you.

Reading

A. Discuss these questions with a partner.

1. What did you like about your elementary school? What didn't you like?
2. What are the most important things for children to learn in elementary school?

B. Choose the correct answer.

1. Southern Cross School is unusual because the classes are ___.
   a. small   c. outdoors
   b. difficult   d. in English

2. The students at Southern Cross study ___ children at other schools.
   a. more subjects than
   b. the same subjects as
   c. different subjects from
   d. fewer subjects than

3. The school hopes that its students will ___ when they get older.
   a. get good jobs   c. work outdoors
   b. attend university d. love nature

4. The students learn about nature in ___ classes.
   a. science   c. math
   b. language   d. all

5. The woman who got the idea for the school was a ___.
   a. parent   c. headmaster
   b. teacher   d. political leader

6. Sue Godding thinks ___ is important for South Africa's future.
   a. teaching new leaders
   b. changing the schools
   c. getting more tourism
   d. changing the economy

Kruger National Park, South Africa

Game-Filled Park Is School for South African Kids

Class time at Southern Cross School, near Kruger National Park in South Africa, is an unusual scene. Teachers and pupils are not shut inside classrooms. Instead, they walk through the grass and bush, or sit in the shade of trees, joined in serious discussion.

The school has the same syllabus that is set for the country's schools by the educational authorities, but the teaching methods are totally different. Southern Cross uses nature as a teaching tool. Classes go outdoors to look for phenomena that can be used to study anything from mathematics and science to language.

Jumbo Williams, the school's headmaster, emphasizes the importance of environmental care. "When students leave school, we want them to be champions of the natural environment," Williams said. "We must make people understand the impact of what we are doing to the environment."

The preschool is set slightly apart from the rest of the school. Today, the first lesson of the day is mathematics. To practice numbers, the children visit the nearby water

trough to look at animal tracks and count how many different animals came to drink during the night. Older students might figure how much water will be used over weeks and months, based on the change in the trough's water levels in one day. "It's amazing how much math is out there," Williams says.

Language, speech, and debate classes focus on conservation issues. A recent student debate centered on whether people should give water to animals in the wild. In another example, finding a dead animal could lead to an investigation of how and why it died.

The idea for the school came from Sue Godding, who was the manager of a game lodge next to Kruger National Park. When her children reached school age, she decided to start a school that offered a top-quality education in a natural environment. Southern Cross opened in January 2002 with 40 children. More than 250 people applied for jobs as teachers. Today, enrollment is over 100.

Godding says nature-based tourism is one of South Africa's national treasures. She believes that the country needs to produce people who understand the environment and the need to preserve it. "We need leaders in all fields who, when they make an important decision, can do so with a sound knowledge of how this world is to survive," she says.

Engage!

In your opinion, are the students at Southern Cross School getting a good education?

C. Write the underlined words from the article next to their meanings.

1. _____ wild animals that are hunted
2. _____ a long narrow container where animals can drink
3. _____ trying to find what happened
4. _____ an outline for all the things that will be taught in a course
5. _____ things that happen
6. _____ a hotel where people stay while they are hunting

Communication

 The Minister of Education in your country has asked your group to make recommendations for improving the country's elementary schools. Make one recommendation in each of these areas. Then explain your ideas to the class.

school buildings   teachers   textbooks
tests   (your own idea)

Writing

How should schools in your country be improved? Write about two different ideas. Explain each idea and give examples.

✓ **Goal 4** | **Propose a new approach to teaching**

Work with two or three students, choose a specific level of education (elementary, secondary, university), a subject (e.g., math, science, geography), and a topic. Prepare a special class with a unique approach. Present your idea to the class.

Before You Watch

England, U.K.

Discuss the questions with a partner.

1. Which country had butlers in the past?
2. Where did butlers work? What did they do?
3. Have you ever seen a butler in a movie or TV show? Describe the character.

While You Watch

A. Watch the video *Butler School* and circle the answers.

1. The students come from (the same/many) countries.
2. The students think the course is (difficult/fun).
3. The students learn to be a butler by (practicing/reading).

B. What does a student learn at this school? Watch again and check the things they study.

	✓
1. how to walk correctly	
2. how to drive a car	
3. how to stop a thief	
4. what to say to a king	
5. how to cook expensive food	
6. how to speak English	
7. what to say on the telephone	
8. how to iron a newspaper	

 C. Watch the video again and fill in the missing words.

1. So in modern England, where does one _____ a good butler?
2. Seventy years ago, there were an estimated _____ thousand butlers.
3. Ivor Spencer wants to use his school _____ to bring back the butler to this land of _____.
4. Over the next five weeks, _____ students from countries such as Spain and Canada will have _____ lessons in the art of being a butler.
5. On every course there are about two people that don't make it past the first _____ days.
6. By the third _____ of the course, the students start to find out if they really can become butlers or not.
7. Now they are butlers and they are part of a very old English _____.

After You Watch

 Role-play this situation.

Student A: You are a wealthy businessman or businesswoman who needs a butler.
Student B: You have graduated from butler school, and you are applying for a job in the home of Student A.

Communication

Make a magazine advertisement for a butler school. Include information on a butler's work, what students will learn at the school, and why being a butler is a good job. Decorate your ad with drawings.

SPACE

1. What is the best caption for each photo?
   a. a rocket launch
   b. an image of space
   c. astronauts
   d. unmanned space exploration

2. What's been in the news recently about space?

UNIT GOALS

Talk about the future
Consider the realities of living in space
Discuss the future of space exploration
Summarize a sequence of events

▲ *Sputnik* was the first man-made satellite to orbit Earth.

▲ Astronaut Edwin Aldrin walks on the Moon.

Vocabulary

A. Read the article.

> ### Space Exploration
>
> The space age began in 1957, when Russia put the **satellite** *Sputnik* into **orbit** around the Earth. Since that time, human beings have explored the **universe** with **manned missions** to the moon and **unmanned** space probes to Mars, Jupiter, and other **planets**. We have **discovered** much about the objects in space and about human beings' ability to live in space. This knowledge has changed some people's ideas about **colonizing** the moon or Mars, while others continue to dream about this possibility.

B. Write each word in **blue** separately next to the correct meaning.

1. with people onboard _____
2. the process of exploring; looking for new things _____
3. to become aware of or learn something new _____
4. the whole of space and all the planets, stars, and so on _____
5. without people onboard _____
6. large objects such as Earth or Saturn that moves around a star _____
7. a man-made object in space that moves around the Earth _____
8. a curved path in space around a planet, moon, or star _____
9. the act of populating a new place such as the moon _____
10. a special journey or task _____

Grammar: The future

Be going to and will	Present progressive tense	Simple present tense

* We use both *be going to* and *will* to talk about the future.
 	
   NASA **is going to** have more unmanned missions in the future.
 	
   A new telescope **will** be introduced next year.
 	
* *Will* is used for sudden decisions.
   *Is that tea? I***'ll** have some, please.*
	* We can use the present progressive tense to talk about definite future plans.
	
	   Joyce and Walter **are flying** to Mexico City next month.
	
	   Their friends **are picking** them up at the airport.
		* We sometimes use the simple present tense to talk about scheduled events in the future.
		
		   Our train **leaves** at 8:30 a.m.
		
		   The movie **starts** in five minutes.

A. Read the email message from a student to her former teacher. Underline the expressions that refer to the future.

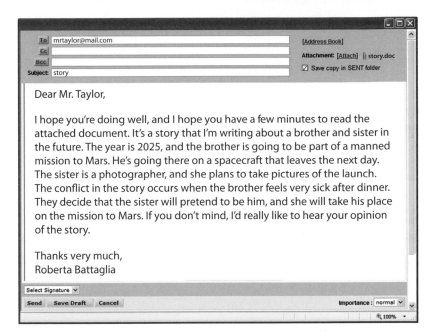

To: mrtaylor@mail.com
Cc:
Bcc:
Subject: story

[Address Book]
Attachment: [Attach] story.doc
☑ Save copy in SENT folder

Dear Mr. Taylor,

I hope you're doing well, and I hope you have a few minutes to read the attached document. It's a story that I'm writing about a brother and sister in the future. The year is 2025, and the brother is going to be part of a manned mission to Mars. He's going there on a spacecraft that leaves the next day. The sister is a photographer, and she plans to take pictures of the launch. The conflict in the story occurs when the brother feels very sick after dinner. They decide that the sister will pretend to be him, and she will take his place on the mission to Mars. If you don't mind, I'd really like to hear your opinion of the story.

Thanks very much,
Roberta Battaglia

Select Signature ▼
Send   Save Draft   Cancel   Importance : normal ▼
🔍 100% ▾

B. What will these be like in the future? Make predictions with *be going to* and *will*.

| transportation | the environment | communication | food |

Conversation

Track 2-25

A. Close your book and listen to the conversation. When does the training program start?

Tina: Alex, what are you going to do after high school?
Alex: Whoa! I don't even know what I'm doing after school today!
Tina: Very funny. I'm going to enroll in a training program.
Alex: What kind of training program?
Tina: They teach you to be a laboratory assistant. It doesn't take very long, and it starts a week after graduation.
Alex: That sounds all right. And what will you do when you finish the program?
Tina: I'll look for a job in a scientific laboratory. All of them need lab assistants.
Alex: That's a pretty good idea. Eric is joining the military when he graduates.
Tina: So everybody has a plan except you.
Alex: True. That's what I'll do after school today! I'll plan my future!

B. Practice the conversation with a partner. Switch roles and practice it again.

✓ Goal 1   Talk about the future

Think about your own future. Tell your partner what you will probably do in:
- the immediate future (this afternoon, tonight, tomorrow).
- the near future (next month, next year, after you graduate).
- the more distant future (in five years, in ten years, when you retire).

Listening

Track 2-26

A. Listen to a radio interview with an astronaut. Check the things she has done.

☐ studied botany (the science of plants)
☐ conducted experiments onboard the International Space Station
☐ made repairs outside the International Space Station
☐ slept attached to a wall of the International Space Station
☐ returned to Earth

Track 2-26

B. Listen again and fill in the chart.

Plants involved in Wilma Foster's experiments:	
Exciting aspects of life onboard the International Space Station:	
Difficult aspects of life onboard the International Space Station:	

 C. Discuss these questions with a partner.

1. Why do you think Dr. Foster wants to return to the International Space Station?
2. Why are the results of experiments conducted in space important?

Engage!

In what ways does space exploration benefit human beings? Do those benefits outweigh the costs of space exploration?

Pronunciation: Stress in compound nouns

A. Listen to and repeat the words. Notice how the stress is on the first part of each compound noun.

Track 2-27

> **spacecraft backpack lifesaver hardware bedroom**

B. Some compound nouns are written as two words, and some are hyphenated. Listen to and repeat the words.

Track 2-27

> **space walk fruit juice space station follow-up check-in**

C. Fill in each blank with a compound noun from exercises **A** and **B**. Then compare your answers with a partner's and take turns reading the sentences aloud.

1. I'm thirsty! Do we have any _____?
2. The _____ orbits the Earth.
3. That study guide was a real _____! I might not have passed the exam without it.
4. I think it would be difficult to sleep without a _____.
5. After you're treated at the hospital, you might need to return for a _____.
6. Hector left his _____ at home, and all his books were in it!

Communication

A. Imagine that your group is going to be part of a mission to the International Space Station. Decide what kind of scientific experiments you will do. Then make a list of everything you will need to take onboard the station in order to conduct your experiments.

B. Do a short presentation for the class. Talk about your plans for the space station mission and explain the items on your list.

 Goal 2 **Consider the realities of living in space**

Would you enjoy living and working aboard the International Space Station? Explain to a partner why you would or would not want to be an astronaut.

Word Focus

Scientists **conduct experiments**.

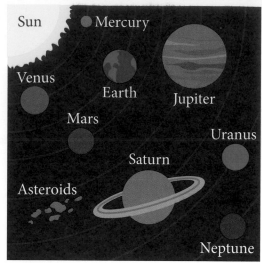

Sun   ● Mercury

Venus

Earth

Jupiter

Mars

Uranus

Saturn

Asteroids

Neptune

Language Expansion: Future time expressions

Track 2-28

A. Listen to two university professors. Underline the time expressions when you hear them.

Speaker A

in a little while

one day

in 10 years

Speaker B

someday soon

one of these days

sooner or later

Track 2-28

B. Listen again to Speaker A and make a simple time line. Which event happens the soonest? Which happens in the more distant future?

Track 2-28

C. Listen again to Speaker B. Which two events is the speaker less certain about? Which event is she more certain about? How do you know?

Grammar: Future modals

Modals for speculating

* When we speculate or make guesses about the future, we use *may, might,* or *could.*
    *Mrs. Lawrence **may** teach part-time next year.*
    *The launch **might** not be delayed this time.*
    *All of this **could** happen within our lifetime.*

Modals of ability and necessity

*We do not use single-word modals with *will* or *be going to.*
    Incorrect: *People **will can** live on Mars someday.*
    *Sherry **is going to must** take Physics 322 sooner or later.*
* Instead, we use *be able to* for necessity and *have to* or *need to* for necessity.
    Correct: *I **am** not **going to be able to** call you tomorrow.*
    *Scientists **will have to** solve this problem some day soon.*
    *You **are going to need to** get a passport.*

A. Fill in the blank with any appropriate modal expression from the chart.

1. In the near future, people will _____ live longer than they can now.
2. More women _____ run for president in future elections.
3. I'm sure I'm going to _____ pay a lot for the jacket I want.
4. Do you think people _____ live on the moon someday?
5. According to the news, we _____ have a very hot summer.

B. On a piece of paper, write answers to the questions using modals from the chart.

1. What do you think people will be wearing in 2050?
2. What do you think transportation will be like in 20 years?
3. When do you think people will be able to travel to Mars?
4. What do you think people are going to need to take to Mars?
5. What kinds of new jobs do you think there will be in the future?

 C. Take turns asking the questions and sharing your answers from exercise **B**.

Conversation

Track 2-29 **A.** Close your book and listen to the conversation. Which speaker is the most convincing to you?

Jacob:	What do you think? Will people ever walk on the moon again?
Matthew:	I don't know. They might, but there are still problems with the technology.
Jacob:	Do you mean the space shuttle accidents?
Matthew:	Of course. It's risky to send people into space.
Jacob:	That's true, but it's the only way to experience the moon firsthand.
Matthew:	Sure, but unmanned spacecraft can travel much farther than the moon.
Jacob:	And there are going to be technical problems with those missions, too.
Matthew:	OK, any future space exploration could have technical problems.
Jacob:	But a human being could repair equipment and solve problems!
Matthew:	You're right. Maybe I'll get lucky and they'll send you into space.

 B. Practice the conversation with a partner. Switch roles and practice it again.

Real Language

You can disagree with someone politely by saying, *That's true, but . . .*

Goal 3 **Discuss the future of space exploration**

Talk in a small group. What kind of space exploration is happening now?
What will space exploration be like in the near future and the distant future?

Reading

A. How quickly can you find the answers in the article?

1. In what year was the Hubble Space Telescope launched? _____

2. Why is Earth's atmosphere a problem for astronomers? _____

3. What did Lyman Spitzer propose? _____

4. What kind of object was Shoemaker-Levy? _____

5. When was the final Hubble service mission completed? _____

B. Circle **T** for *true*, **F** for *false*, or **NI** for *no information* (if the answer is not in the reading).

1. The best telescopes on Earth are not affected by the atmosphere.   T   F   NI

2. Lyman Spitzer was Russian.   T   F   NI

3. Spitzer thought the orbiting telescope would mainly add to the scientific ideas that already existed.   T   F   NI

4. Hubble has confirmed that black holes really exist.   T   F   NI

5. The universe is expanding more quickly than it used to.   T   F   NI

□ Space

The Hubble Space Telescope

For centuries, astronomers looking at the moon, the planets, and the stars have faced a basic problem: the earth's atmosphere. Although it provides the air we breathe and protection from the sun, the atmosphere interferes with astronomers' ability to see into space—even with the largest and most sophisticated telescopes.

Then came Lyman Spitzer, an astrophysicist with a remarkable idea: Put a large telescope in orbit around the earth, *outside* of the earth's atmosphere. Spitzer proposed this idea in 1946, 11 years before Russia launched the world's first man-made satellite and long before technology such as microprocessors, digital imaging, or the space shuttle existed. Spitzer claimed the telescope would serve not just to test and refine existing ideas, but also to spark entirely new ones. "The chief contribution of such a radically new and more powerful instrument," he predicted, "would be, not to supplement our present ideas of the universe we live in, but rather to uncover new **phenomena** not yet imagined, and perhaps to **modify** profoundly our basic concepts of space and time."

Spitzer was right. In 1993, NASA released the first images from the Hubble telescope. Since then, scientists have used Hubble to follow the impact of the 1994 comet Shoemaker-Levy 9 into the atmosphere of the giant planet Jupiter. They have produced images of the astonishing and unique beauty of planetary nebulae—the shells of gas produced by unstable, dying stars. They have proved the existence of black holes at the centers of galaxies. And just as Spitzer predicted, Hubble has provided new information that changes our ideas about the universe.

Astronomers already knew that the universe was **expanding**, but they expected this expansion to be slowing down due to the gravity of all the **matter** in the universe, just as a ball thrown into the air falls back to Earth. Instead, astronomers discovered that cosmic expansion is not slowing down at all—it is speeding up! It is as if a ball, thrown into the air, at first slowed but then sped up and simply flew away. No natural **force** on Earth can do this, but some kind of energy must be causing the **acceleration**.

Scientists are calling this unknown force *dark energy* and are working to learn more about it. However, Hubble is getting old, and its final scheduled service mission was completed in 2008. Fortunately, other orbiting telescopes such as the Spitzer Space Telescope and the Chandra X-ray Observatory are sending information to Earth, and the gigantic James Webb Space Telescope is scheduled for launch in 2013. Webb will gather infrared light with a mirror over 21 feet (6.4 meters) in diameter! Together with a growing network of ground-based telescopes and detectors, these space observatories promise, as Lyman Spitzer noted back in 1946, to alter not only what we know, but how we learn.

Word Focus

phenomena = natural events or conditions
modify = change
expanding = becoming larger, moving outward
matter = physical substances: solids, liquids, and gases
force = power
acceleration = going faster and faster

Writing

A. Number the following in chronological order.

_____ The James Webb telescope is launched.
_____ Spitzer proposes his idea.
_____ Astronomers make a surprising discovery about the universe's expansion.
_____ Early astronomers are limited by the atmosphere.
_____ The Hubble telescope is launched.
_____ Astronomers view beautiful images from Hubble.
_____ Human beings continue to learn more about the universe.

B. Write a three-paragraph composition about the past, present, and future of orbiting telescopes. Use information from the article and exercise **A**. Use your own words as much as possible.

C. Share your composition with a partner. Give each other suggestions for improvement.

Goal 4 **Summarize a sequence of events**

Make a list of important events in your life and some of your future plans. Tell a partner about your own past, present, and future.

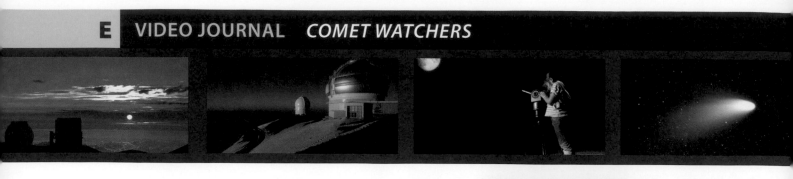

Before You Watch

A. Study the parts of a comet.

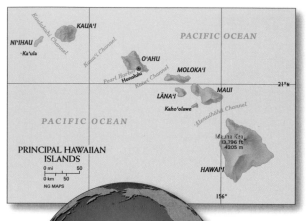

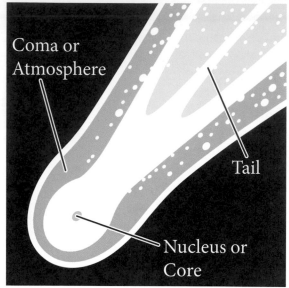

B. Read about Halley's Comet and look up the meanings of the words in **blue**.

Comets are defined as small objects that orbit the sun, but for astronomers, comets are much more exciting than that. Halley's Comet, for example, has a 76-year orbit, so most people only see it once in a lifetime. And when Halley does come around, professional and **amateur** astronomers jump at the opportunity to view the comet.

Mauna Kea in Hawaii is the Earth's highest **volcano**, and with its thin, dry atmosphere it's one of the best places for telescopes. To study Halley's Comet, scientists use ordinary telescopes, but also telescopes that can "see" **infrared** light. Some space agencies also send unmanned probes to measure the size, the temperature, and the **composition** of the comet.

One interesting thing about comets is that they only have a tail when they're near the sun. Despite appearances, the tail is not caused by the comet's movement, but by the **solar wind** pushing the comet's atmosphere away.

While You Watch

A. Watch the video and circle each word when you hear it. (Some words are used more than once.)

amateur	**core**	**solar wind**	
atmosphere	**infrared**	**tail**	
coma	**nucleus**	**volcano**	**composition**

 B. Watch the video again and match the statements to the people who might make them.

a. a representative from the European Space Agency

b. Dale Cruikshank, a comet specialist at the University of Hawaii

c. an amateur astronomer

d. Ron, an infrared specialist

1. I don't know much about astronomy, but I'm excited about seeing Halley's Comet once in my lifetime. ____

2. Our "Giotto" probe got closer to Halley's Comet than any other probe. ____

3. The photographs I'm taking with this telescope are the best way to view very large objects in space. ____

4. I'm measuring the heat radiation from Halley's Comet in order to learn more about its temperature and composition. ____

▲ the spectacular Hale-Bopp Comet

▲ the 1066 appearance of Halley's Comet

After you Watch

 Why do people become amateur or professional astronomers?
Make a list of reasons people enjoy star-gazing.

Communication

You are graduate students at a major university working on your PhD degree in astronomy. Next year, a comet will be close to Earth, and you want to study it. Write a letter to the head of your department requesting money for a trip to Hawaii. Be sure to explain why Hawaii is the best place to do your research.

Unit 1 People and Places

ancient: very old; from an earlier time

arid: describes places that receive very little rain

employment: having a job

fishing: catching fish

frigid: describes extremely cold places

herding: caring for a group of animals such as cattle or sheep

hunting: killing wild animals for food

inhabit: to live in a place

migration: moving from one part of the world to another

occur: to happen

political: relating to the way power is achieved or used in a society

rainy: describes places that receive a large amount of rain

sail: to move across water in a boat using the wind

snowy: describes places that receive a large amount of snow

temperate: describes places with distinct seasons that are never extremely hot or cold

tropical: describes hot, humid places near the earth's equator

Unit 2 The Mind

cell: the smallest part of an animal or plant

compare: see how two things are similar or different

concentrate: think very hard about something

conclusion: something you decide after looking at all the information

experiment: a scientific test to see if something is true

hearing: your ability to sense sounds

laboratory: a place where scientists work

memorize: learn so that you can remember exactly

memory: your ability to remember things

mental : in your mind

portion: part

react: speak or move when something happens

research: studying something to discover new facts about it

results: the information that scientists get after an experiment

retain: keep, continue to have

sight: your ability to see

smell: your ability to sense the odor of things

survey: collecting information by asking many people the same questions

taste: your ability to sense the flavor of things

technique: a way to do an activity

theory: a scientific idea

touch: your ability to sense how things feel

visualize: make a picture in your mind

Unit 3 Changing Planet

climate change: a change in the normal weather patterns

coal: a black mineral made of carbon taken from the ground

conservation: saving and protecting the environment

deforestation: the cutting down of trees over a large area

extreme: very great in degree or intensity

global warming: a gradual rise in the earth's temperature

increase: the number, level, or amount becoming greater

invasive species: plants and animals with no local natural controls on their populations

oil: a thick liquid found underground and used as a fuel

polar ice: ice at the north and south polar regions of Earth

sea level: the average level of the ocean

storm: heavy rain or snow with strong winds

temperature: how hot or cold something is

Unit 4 Money

ATM: automatic teller machine (a machine that dispenses money)

bargain: something good for a low price

borrow: get money that you will give back in the future

budget: a plan for spending your money

cash: money in coins and bills

checking account: a bank account that you write checks from

deposit: put money into a bank

expenses: money that you spend

in debt: owing money to a bank or a company

income: money that you receive for working

lend: give money to another person that they will give back in the future

PIN number: personal identification number (secret number)

receipt: a paper that shows how much money you have paid or given

savings account: a bank account where you save money to spend later

teller: a person who works in a bank

withdraw: take money out of the bank

Unit 5 Survival

banned: not allowed

cope: deal with something successfully

ecosystem: all the plants and animals in a certain area

emergency: a bad situation that requires immediate attention

endangered: with *species*, describes one that might become extinct soon

equipment: items needed for a purpose

evacuate: to leave a place because it has become dangerous

first aid: emergency medical treatment

natural disaster: earthquakes, floods, or other damaging natural events

panic: uncontrolled fear in response to danger

predatory: describes an animal that eats other animals

preparation: the process of getting ready

preservation: keeping or maintaining something

reserve: a place where hunting and fishing are not allowed

restore: to return something to the way it was before

situation: the way things are at a certain time

species: a certain kind of plant or animal

supplies: food, equipment, and other things people need

Unit 6 Art

abstract: describes art made with shapes and lines, not pictures of real things

bamboo: a tall tropical plant

brass: a yellow metal made from copper (chemical symbol Cu) and zinc (Zn)

clay: a material made from earth

decorate: make something more attractive by adding to it

designs: a pattern of lines or shapes that is used to decorate something

drawing: a work of art made with a pencil or pen

express: show what you think or feel about something

gold: a very expensive yellow metal (chemical symbol Au)

leather: a material made from animal skin

painting: a work of art made with paint

realistic: describes art that looks like real things

represent: be a symbol for something

sculpture: a work of art made by carving stone, metal, or wood

stained glass: a work of art made with pieces of colored glass

stone: a hard material found in the ground

straw: a material made from dried plants

style: a way of making art that is used by one artist, or a small group

technique: a particular way to do or make something

wood: a material made from trees

Unit 7 Getting Around

board: get on a plane, bus, or ship

connect: come together

destination: the place you are going to

directly: without stopping or changing direction

efficient: not using too much time or energy

fare: money you pay to use public transportation

freight: things that are transported on a vehicle

fuel: a substance like gasoline or oil that is burned to give power

increase: become greater in number or amount

motor vehicle: a car, truck, or bus

pass: a card that shows you have paid to use public transportation for a period of time

passengers: a person who is traveling in a vehicle

pilot: a person who is trained to fly an airplane

reduce: make smaller

route: the way that a train or bus usually goes

speed: how fast something moves

terminal: the end of a train or bus route

ticket: a paper that shows you have paid to use public transportation

transfer: change from one route to another

Unit 8 Competition

athlete: a person who plays sports

championship: a competition to find the best player or team in a sport

cheat: to not obey the rules

coach: someone who trains a person or a sports team

league: a group of teams that play the same sport against each other

loser: the person or team that loses a game or sports event

match: a competition such as a soccer match or tennis match

medal: a metal disk given as a prize in a sports event

points: the numbers that are added together to give the score

score: the total number of points a player or team receives in a sports event

scoreboard: a large sign that shows the score during a sports event

sportsmanship: polite behavior during a sports event

team: a group of people who compete together

training: learning and practicing a sport

trophy: a prize such as a cup given to the winner of a competition

winner: the person or team that wins a game or sports event

Unit 9 Danger

attack: try to hurt someone's body

bite: use your teeth to cut through something

estimate: guess about the number or amount of something

injured: hurt a person's body

poison: something that kills people if they eat or drink it

prevent: make sure that something doesn't happen

risk: possibility that something bad will happen

scratch: use claws or fingernails to hurt

sting: make a hole in the skin and put poison inside

substance: a solid, liquid, or gas

survive: live through a dangerous situation

toxic: containing poison

Unit 10 Mysteries

construct: to build, make, or create something

evidence: clues that make you believe something is true

figure out: to solve or understand something

investigate: to try to find out what happened or what is true

prehistoric: describes people or things that existed before information was written down

remains: the parts of something that are left after most of it is gone

search: to look carefully for something or someone

speculate: to make guesses about something

Unit 11 Learning

agriculture: the study of farming

apply: fill out a form to ask for something

business: the study of how companies work

campus: an area of land with college or university buildings

chemistry: the science of substances and how they react together

course: a series of lessons or lectures about a subject

deadline: the last day to do something

demonstration: showing something

economics: the study of money

education: the study of ways to teach and learn

engineering: the study of how to build and make things

enroll: join a school or a class

geology: the science of earth and rocks

law: the study of how laws work

lecture: a speech

major: main subject that you are studying

practical experience: learning by doing something yourself

psychology: the science of the mind

requirement: something that you must have or do to be suitable for something

scholarship: money given to good students to pay for their studies

semester: half of a school year

social work: the study of how to give help and advice to people with social problems

study tour: a trip to learn about a subject

tuition: money you pay to study

Unit 12 Space

astronaut: a person who goes into outer space

colonize: the act of populating a new place such as the Moon

discover: to become aware of or learn something new

exploration: the process of exploring; looking for new things

image: a picture

launch: to send up into the air

manned: with people onboard

mission: a special journey or task

orbit: a curved path in space around a planet, moon, or star

planet: a large object such as Earth or Saturn that moves around a star

rocket: a space vehicle that is shaped like a long tube

satellite: a man-made object in space that moves around Earth

universe: the whole of space and all the planets, stars, etc.

unmanned: without people onboard

TEXT

10–11 Adapted from "Pioneers of the Pacific," by Roff Smith: National Geographic Magazine, March 2008; **16, 20, 22–23** Adapted from "Beyond the Brain," by James Shreeve: National Geographic Magazine, March 2005; **34–35** Adapted from "Carbon's New Math," by Bill McKibben: National Geographic Magazine, October 2007; **46–47** Adapted from "The Power of Money," by Peter T. White: National Geographic Magazine, January 1993; **56** Adapted from "Blue Haven," by Kennedy Warne: National Geographic Magazine, April, 2007; **64** Adapted from "Masters of Traditional Arts," by Marjorie Hunt and Boris Weintraub: National Geographic Magazine, January 1991; **70–71** Adapted from "Los Angeles Restoring Its Freeway Murals," by Stefan Lovgren: National Geographic News, July 17, 2003; **76** Adapted from "The Future of Flying," by Michael Klesius: National Geographic Magazine, December 2003; **82–83** Adapted from "Last Days of the Rickshaws," by Calvin Trillin: National Geographic Magazine, April 2008; **94–95** Adapted from "In Sports Red is Winning Color Study Says," by John Roach: National Geographic News, May 18, 2005; **102** (Listening Text), **106–107** Adapted from "Pick Your Poison," by Cathy Newman: National Geographic Magazine, May 2005; **118–119** Adapted from "Hands Across Time," by Luc-Henri Fage: National Geographic Magazine, August 2005; **130–131** Adapted from "Game-Filled Park Is School for South African Kids," by Leon Marshall: National Geographic News, January 31, 2005; **136** Adapted from "The Space Age at 50," by Guy Gugliotta: National Geographic Magazine, October 2007; **142–143** Adapted from "Hubble Vision," by Timothy Ferris: National Geographic Magazine, November 2007

ILLUSTRATION

iv–v, 8, 11, 12: National Geographic Maps; **18:** Nesbitt Graphics, Inc.; **32:** National Geographic Maps; **36:** (t) National Geographic Maps, (b) Nesbitt Graphics, Inc.; **42:** (t) National Geographic Maps, (b) Ted Hammond/IllustrationOnline.com; **44:** (all) Nesbitt Graphics, Inc.; **46:** Ted Hammond/IllustrationOnline.com; **48:** National Geographic Maps; **55:** Ted Hammond/IllustrationOnline.com; **56, 58, 60:** National Geographic Maps; **68:** Keith Neely/IllustrationOnLine.com; **72:** National Geographic Maps; **80:** (all) Nesbitt Graphics, Inc.; **82, 84:** National Geographic Maps; **90:** Nesbitt Graphics, Inc.; **92:** Ted Hammond/IllustrationOnline.com; **93:** Nesbitt Graphics, Inc.; **94, 102:** National Geographic Maps; **104:** (all) Ralph Voltz/IllustrationOnLine.com; **106:** Keith Neely/IllustrationOnLine.com; **116:** National Geographic Maps **117:** Nesbitt Graphics, Inc.; **119, 120, 130, 132:** National Geographic Maps; **137:** Nesbitt Graphics, Inc.; **140:** Jim Atherton; **144:** (l) National Geographic Maps, (r) Jim Atherton.

PHOTO

Cover photo: Justin Guariglia/National Geographic Image Collection.

iv: (t) Elisa Cicinelli/AGE Fotostock; (ml) Stephan Hoerold/iStockphoto, (mr) Forest Woodward/iStockphoto, (b) Gordon Wiltsie/National Geographic Image Collection; **v:** (tr) George Cairns/iStockphoto, (ml) Palani Mohan/National Geographic Image Collection, (mr) Katarzyna Mazurowska/iStockphoto, (b) Medford Taylor/National Geographic Image Collection; **2–3:** (l to r) Ira Block/National Geographic Image Collection, Jim Richardson/National Geographic Image Collection, Lynn Johnson/National Geographic Image Collection, Bates Littlehales/National Geographic Image Collection; **4:** (t) David Boyer/National Geographic Image Collection, (b) Christina Richards/Shutterstock; **5:** Ljupco Smokovski/Shutterstock; **6:** (l to r) David Edwards/National Geographic Image Collection, iStockphoto, Andrew Rich/iStockphoto, Leigh Schindler/iStockphoto; **7:** Catherine Yeulet/iStockphoto; **8:** (l to r) Thomas J. Abercrombie/National Geographic Image Collection, Michael Melford/National Geographic Image Collection, Michael Nichols/National Geographic Image Collection, James Forte/National Geographic Image Collection, Richard Nowitz/National Geographic Image Collection; **9:** Andresr/Shutterstock; **10:** (t, both) Stephen Alvarez/National Geographic Image Collection, (b) J.D.Heaton/AGE Fotostock; **12–13:** (l to r) Jenny Solomon/Shutterstock, Jon Tarrant/iStockphoto, Elisa Cicinelli/AGE Fotostock, Constant44/Shutterstock, iStockphoto, Natalia Bratslavsky/Shutterstock, Elisa Cicinelli/AGE Fotostock, Jenny Solomon/Shutterstock; **12:** (b) Brian Adducci/iStockphoto; **13:** (m) Ty Milford/Getty Images, (b) Anna Chelnokova/Shutterstock; **14–15:** (l to r) Felix Mizioznikov/iStockphoto, Richard Nowitz/National Geographic Image Collection (2), Panoramic Images/Getty Images; **16:** (t) Peter Baxter/Shutterstock, (b) Cary Wolinsky/National Geographic Image Collection; **19:** (tl) Mark Coffey/iStockphoto, (tr) Peter Widmann/AGE Fotostock, (b) Sandro Donda/Shutterstock; **20:** (t) Alan Merrigan/Shutterstock, (b) Cary Wolinsky/National Geographic Image

Collection; **21:** (l to r) Sigapo/Shutterstock, Creasence/Shutterstock, Simon Askham/iStockphoto; **22:** (all) Cary Wolinsky/National Geographic Image Collection; **24–25:** (l to r) iStockphoto, Andrew Rich/iStockphoto, Rob Marmion/Shutterstock, Olga Zaporozhskaya/Shutterstock, Anatomical Design/Shutterstock, iStockphoto, Rob Marmion/Shutterstock, iStockphoto; **24:** (m) Sebastian Kaulitzki/Shutterstock, (b) ajt/Shutterstock; **25:** (b) Tatiana Popova/Shutterstock; **26–27:** (l to r) Gordon Wiltsie/National Geographic Image Collection, James P. Blair/National Geographic Image Collection, Tyrone Turner/National Geographic Image Collection, Sarah Leen/National Geographic Image Collection; **28:** (t) Mattias Klum/National Geographic Image Collection, (b) Jodi Cobb/National Geographic Image Collection; **29:** Gideon Mendel/Impact/HIP/The Image Works; **30:** (t) Digital Vision/Getty Images, (middle, l to r) NOAA, Gordon Gahan/National Geographic Image Collection, Narinder Nanu/AFP/Getty Images, Michel Spingler/AP Images; **32:** Mark Jones/Photolibrary; **33:** Tim Laman/National Geographic Image Collection; **34:** (tl) Dwight Nadig/iStockphoto, (br) Sarah Leen/National Geographic Image Collection; **35:** Annie Griffiths Belt/National Geographic Image Collection; **36–37:** (l to r) Regien Paassen/Shutterstock, Jaap Hart/iStockphoto, Picture Partners/Alamy, Klaas Lingbeek- van Kranen/iStockphoto, Katarzyna Mazurowska/iStockphoto, Inge Schepers/Shutterstock, Klaas Lingbeek- van Kranen/iStockphoto, Regien Paassen/Shutterstock; **37:** (m) Katarzyna Mazurowska/Shutterstock. (b) Eric Gevaert/Shutterstock; **38–39:** (l to r) Maxim Tupikov/Shutterstock, Joel Blit/iStockphoto, Zhuda/Shutterstock, Sakchai Lalit/AP Images; **40:** Joel Blit/iStockphoto; **41:** Digital Vision/Getty Images; **43:** Galina Barskaya/Shutterstock; **45:** Ross Pictures/JupiterImages; **47:** Bob Bird/AP Images; **48–49:** (l to r) Palani Mohan/National Geographic Image Collection, JCVStock/Shutterstock, Symphonie/Getty Images, Vladimir Melnik/Shutterstock, Annie Griffiths Belt/National Geographic Image Collection, Stuart Dee/Getty Images, JCVStock/Shutterstock, Vladimir Melnik/Shutterstock; **48:** (m) Abraham Nowitz/National Geographic

Image Collection; **49:** (m) Stuart Dee/Getty Images, (b) Palani Mohan/National Geographic Image Collection; **50–51:** (l to r) Mark Thiessen/National Geographic Image Collection, Stephen Alvarez/National Geographic Image Collection, Reza/National Geographic Image Collection, Lowell Georgia/National Geographic Image Collection; **52:** ZTS/Shutterstock; **53:** (t) Joel Sartore/National Geographic Image Collection, (b) iStockphoto; **54:** (t) TatjanaRittner/Shutterstock, (b) PhotostoGo.com; **56:** Brian J. Skerry/National Geographic Image Collection; **57:** Mattias Klum/National Geographic Image Collection; **58:** (tl) Tom Vezo/Minden Pictures/National Geographic Image Collection, (br) Josh Bernstein/BOSS, Inc.; **59:** Josh Bernstein/BOSS, Inc.; **60–61:** (l to r) Carsten Peter/National Geographic Image Collection, Gordon Wiltsie/National Geographic Image Collection, Ralph Lee Hopkins/National Geographic Image Collection, Bates Littlehales/National Geographic Image Collection, Carsten Peter/National Geographic Image Collection, Bates Littlehales/National Geographic Image Collection, Ralph Lee Hopkins/National Geographic Image Collection, Carsten Peter/National Geographic Image Collection; **60:** (m) Bates Littlehales/National Geographic Image Collection, (b) Małgorzata Ostrowska/iStockphoto; **62–63:** (l to r) photos.com, Boris Shapiro/iStockphoto, The London Art Archive/Alamy, Musée d'Orsay Paris/Gianni Dagli Orti/The Art Archive; **64:** (t) David Alan Harvey/Magnum Photos, (bottom, l to r) Hsing-Wen Hsu/iStockphoto, Patricia Hofmeester/Shutterstock, Rachel Donahue/iStockphoto; **65:** (t) George Ostertag/SuperStock, (b) Jorge Felix Costa/Shutterstock; **66:** (a) epa/Corbis, (b) Städtische Galerie im Lenbachhaus Munich/Alfredo Dagli Orti/The Art Archive, (c) Muskopf, Michael Todd/SuperStock, (d) Victoria and Albert Museum London/Eileen Tweedy/The Art Archive, (e) Fine Art Photographic Library/SuperStock; **67:** iStockphoto; **68:** (1) Maceofoto/Shutterstock, (2) photos.com, (3) Maxstockphoto/Shutterstock, (4) photos.com, (5) Najin/Shutterstock, (6) Zastol`skiy Victor Leonidovich/Shutterstock, (7) Eky Chan/Shutterstock, (8) Pomah/Shutterstock; **70:** Kord.com/AGE Fotostock; **71:** Chris Cheadle/Alamy;

72–73: (l to r) Robert B. Goodman/National Geographic Image Collection, Howell Walker/National Geographic Image Collection, Medford Taylor/National Geographic Image Collection, Charles Allmon/National Geographic Image Collection, Kenneth MacLeish/National Geographic Image Collection, Belinda Wright/National Geographic Image Collection, Howell Walker/National Geographic Image Collection, Kenneth MacLeish/National Geographic Image Collection; **72:** (b) Howell Walker/National Geographic Image Collection; **73:** (b) Charles Allmon/National Geographic Image Collection; **74–75:** (l to r) Thomas Nord/Shutterstock, Johannes Compaan/Shutterstock, Natalia Bratslavsky/Shutterstock, Fritz Hoffmann/National Geographic Image Collection; **76:** Lushpix Illustration/AGE Fotostock; **77:** (t) William Attard McCarthy/Shutterstock, (m) Maigi/Shutterstock, (b) Marka/AGE Fotostock; **78:** (l to r) Dan Moore/iStockphoto, Markrhiggins/Shutterstock, Qing Ding/Shutterstock; **79:** Barbara Miller/iStockphoto; **80:** Marion Kaplan/Alamy; **81:** Tom Bonaventure/Getty Images; **83:** Ami Vitale/National Geographic Image Collection; **84–85:** (l to r) Rafal Dudziec/iStockphoto, iStockphoto, David P. Smith/Shutterstock, Jason Verschoor/iStockphoto, PhotostoGo.com, Gary718/Shutterstock, Rafal Dudziec/iStockphoto, Gary718/Shutterstock; **84:** (b) Rafal Dudziec/iStockphoto; **85:** (m) Gary718/Shutterstock, (b) PhotostoGo.com; **86–87:** (l to r) Afaizal/Shutterstock, Walter Quirtmair/Shutterstock, Al Bello/Getty Images, Mojgan Ramezani/Getty Images; **88:** Gene Chutka/iStockphoto; **89:** (t) Chris Schmidt/iStockphoto, (b) James P. Blair/National Geographic Image Collection; **90:** (t) iStockphoto, (b) J. Baylor Roberts/National Geographic Image Collection; **91:** photos.com; **93:** Iurii Konoval/Shutterstock; **94:** Kate Thompson/National Geographic Image Collection; **95:** Cyril Ruoso/Minden Pictures/National Geographic Image Collection; **96–97:** (l to r) Sergei Bachlakov/Shutterstock, Forest Woodward/iStockphoto, Diane Garcia/iStockphoto, Brian Poirier/iStockphoto, Sergei Bachlakov/Shutterstock, Cynthia Baldauf/iStockphoto, Forest Woodward/iStockphoto, Sergei Bachlakov/Shutterstock; **96:** (m & b)